S0-ABZ-311

THE WORM FORGIVES THE PLOUGH

By the same Author

SHAW

FORWARD TO NATURE

FAREWELL TO ARGUMENT

THE SOUNDING CATARACT

IN IRISHMAN'S ENGLAND

AN ARTIST OF LIFE

MARRIAGE AND GENIUS

LEO TOLSTOY

BOUND UPON A COURSE

THE CARLYLES

WHILE FOLLOWING THE PLOUGH

THE TRIUMPH OF THE TREE

THE MOVING WATERS

PATHS OF LIGHT

THE VISION OF GLORY

The Worm Forgives the Plough

'The cut worm forgives the plough'
Proverbs of Hell, William Blake

JOHN STEWART COLLIS

GEORGE BRAZILLER
New York

Published in the United States in 1975 by George Braziller, Inc.

Originally published in England by Charles Knight & Co., Ltd.

For information address the publisher:
George Braziller, Inc.
One Park Avenue, New York 10016

Standard Book Number: 0-8076-0745-2
Library of Congress Catalog Number: 73-92678
Printed in the United States of America
First Printing

ILLUSTRATIONS BY OSCAR RATTI

Contents

Down to Earth

Down to Earth

READING through this book of mine, and subsequent ones of the same kind, I see that my approach has the merit of being highly unoriginal. This is a great asset for me. I need never go out of fashion. For I have never been in the fashion. I am always with it. I came upon the following only a few days ago by John de Dondis, a fourteenth-century sage, who after declaring that he was disinclined to attach too much importance to wholly explicable relationships, added:

> I have learned from long experience that there is nothing that is not marvellous and that the saying of Aristotle is true—that in every natural phenomenon there is something wonderful, nay, in truth, many wonders. We are born and placed among wonders and surrounded by them, so that to whatever object the eye first turns, the same is wonderful and full of wonders, if only we will examine it for a while.

JOHN STEWART COLLIS *1973*

Preface

THE book of Nature lies closed before us. We look round, and everything seems more or less incomprehensible. At least that is my experience. I have come to the stage when, awake at last to the actual existence of the visible world, I also realize the shortness of life, and hasten to acquaint myself with a few of the facts before it is too late and I am dead before I have ever been alive.

The good of it is we can open the book if we choose. That company of devoted and gifted men, called scientific specialists, has placed a great many facts at our disposal. The time has come for me to take advantage of their labours. For many years my approach had been from the other end. For many years I sought for truth, or if you like, God. I did not find it. I found beauty instead. I then understood what was meant by the saying that beauty is truth and truth beauty. I had come to see the whole. Then I was ready to see the part. Now, to-day, I seek the part so as to enhance my vision of the whole. Facts have become my chief stimulus.

I never really got down to the facts until I got down to the earth. I date my resolve and my practice from the time when I became a labourer on the land. It cannot possibly be necessary for everyone, but for me it was essential to come in contact with a thing through work before I could actually see it! Finding myself confronted with the worm or the potato, with the ant or the seed, I was forced to ask myself how much I really knew of these mysteries. Not until I did ask this was I aware that I could hardly answer the simplest question. There may be some others in a like case. If so, they might care to join me.

But I must not pretend that facts are the chief thing about this book, either for myself or for the reader. Quite the contrary. As I have hinted above, facts are fascinating to me only because they heighten my sense of significance. I do not believe in 'the pursuit of knowledge for its own sake'. That phrase strikes me as silly. My pursuit of facts is for the sake of imagination. I always want to relate my physics with metaphysics. This is being very philosophical, you may say. Certainly. Philosophy is the only thing I am fundamentally interested in. For what is a philosopher? Only a man who likes to see the whole. Only a man who refuses to keep things in watertight compartments, and who seeks to relate his knowledge with a vision of life. If this is the poetic attitude also, let us not quarrel with words. There are many facts in this volume—but already I have forgotten most of them. I couldn't pass an examination on them. That doesn't worry me; it is merely a question of memory—which can be refreshed at any minute. The point is I have grasped the facts (and of course I do remember the chief ones). Having grasped them, then thought followed, and emotion followed, and I drew nearer to the mystery. Surely synthesis should be our aim now, and in the future. Only the specialists should specialize. There are now huge wads of knowledge about most things. We should learn to digest it. It is time we learnt to relate our knowledge organically and to see the significance of facts. Knowledge for its own sake is not more worth acquiring than bread for its own sake.

It will be seen from the above remarks and from all the pages that follow, that I stand a long way off from those mystics who declare, with Mr. Aldous Huxley in his *Perennial Philosophy*, that it is only 'in imageless contemplation that the soul comes to the unitive knowledge of reality'. My position is at the side of the contemporary Indian seer, Sri Aurobindo, who claims that 'the touch of Earth is always invigorating to the son of Earth, even when he seeks a supra-physical knowledge'. And he adds that perhaps the metaphysical can only be really mastered in its *fullness* 'when we keep our feet firmly on the physical'. I could not agree more. We are really lost if we fail to make these connections. There is nothing new about it; but to-day our minds should be freer to make the synthesis than when the great mystic Jakob Boehme wrote —'View this world diligently and consider what manner of fruits, sprouts, and branches grow out of the Salitter of the earth, from trees, plants, herbs, roots, flowers, oil, wine, corn, and whatever else there is that thy heart can find out; all is a type of the heavenly pomp.'

Such is the trend of this volume. Nevertheless I have written up to no system—I hope. In setting out on my discoveries I have never aimed to say anything particular, and often have been well content to let the facts speak for themselves. When imagination has stirred and the same thought has flowered on several occasions from different stems, I have been glad to repeat myself, and thus support the view from more than one angle. Consequently there is a considerable degree of subjectivity even in Part One of this book. I can scarcely apologize for the very thing that gives me the necessary heat to pursue my studies and which is in fact my particular contribution. I must leave it to others to popularize science, they do it more thoroughly, and that is not my aim.

In Part Two, when dealing with trees and forestry, my method is still more subjective and reflective. The inquiry called for a technique less taut than in Part One, for a slower pace, and an approach somewhat similar to that of *While Following the Plough.*

A word with regard to Authority. If I used jargon I could afford to be inaccurate, since no one could be quite sure what I had said. Since I like to make things clear, I have been careful to acquire my facts with all the thoroughness and conscientiousness of an ignorant man. This does not mean that sometimes I have not been compelled to choose between two schools of thought, or that the absolutely up-to-date finding is necessarily on my page. I can only claim that I have said nothing without authority, and indeed it will be obvious that many of the facts are too fantastic to have been invented. But when I have felt that a reference was called for, I have given it.

John Stewart Collis

PART ONE

Down to Earth

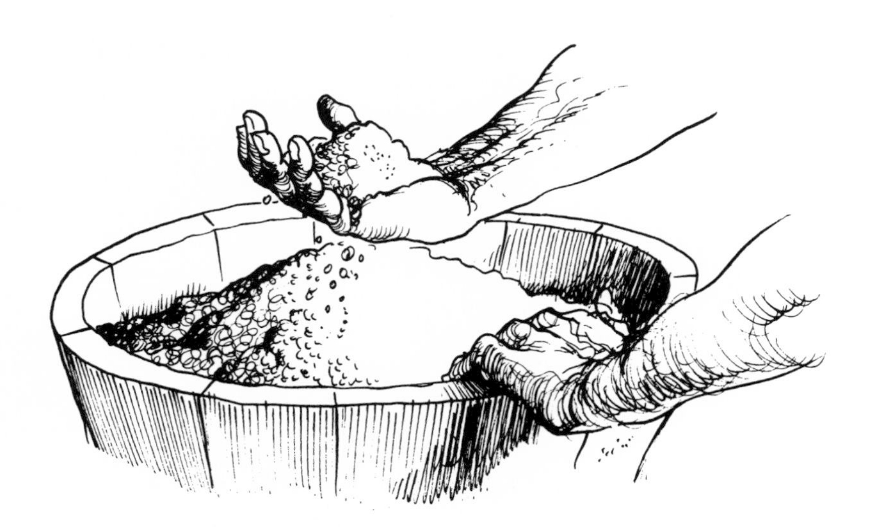

1. THE POTATO

I AM anxious to say a word about the potato. But will the Muse fail me? We sing the flower, we sing the leaf: we seldom sing the seed, the root, the tuber. Indeed the potato enters literature with no very marked success. True, William Cobbett abused it, and Lord Byron made it interesting by rhyming it with Plato; but for the most part it enters politics more easily and has done more to divide England from Ireland than Cromwell himself.

Yet if we praise the potato we praise ourselves, for it is an extreme example of artificiality. 'The earth, in order that she might urge us to labour, the supreme law of life,' says Fabre, 'has been but a harsh stepmother. For the nestling bird she provides abundant food; to us she offers only the fruit of the Bramble and the Blackthorn.' Not everyone realizes this, he said. Some people even imagine that the grape is to-day just like that from which Noah obtained the juice that made him drunk; that the cauliflower, merely with the idea of being pleasant, has of its own accord evolved its creamy-white head; that turnips and carrots, being keenly interested in human affairs, have always of their own motion done their best for man; and that the potato, since the world was young, wishing to please us, has gone through its curious performance. The truth is far otherwise. They were all uneatable at first: it is we who have forced them to become what they now are. 'In its native countries,' says Fabre, 'on the mountains of Chili and Peru, the Potato, in its wild state, is a meagre tubercle, about the size of a Hazel-nut. Man extends the hospitality of his garden to this sorry weed; he plants it in nourishing soil, tends it, waters it, and makes it fruitful with the sweat of his brow. And there, from year to year, the Potato thrives and prospers; it gains in size and nourishing properties, finally becoming a farinaceous tuber the size of our two fists.'

During my first year in the agricultural world I decided to have a good look at the potato and carefully watch its operations. I had never done this before. In fact I had little idea how potatoes actually arrive. With me it is always a question of either knowing a thing or not knowing it, of knowing it from A to Z or not at all; the man who knows a little about everything, from A to B, is incomprehensible to me. Thus I could approach the potato with the clear head of ignorance.

I took one in my hand and offered it my attention. It looked like a smooth stone; a shapeless shape; so dull in appearance that I found it hard to look at it without thinking of something else. I took a knife and cut it in two. It had white flesh extremely like an apple. But it had nothing in the middle, no seed-box, no seeds. How then can it produce more of itself? Well, the season had now come to put it down into the earth. So we planted them into the prepared field, at a distance of one foot from each other—plenty of space in which laboratory they could carry out any work they desired.

In about a fortnight's time I decided to dig up one and see if anything had happened. The first I came to had not changed in appearance at all. From the second, however, two white objects, about the length of a worm, were protruding. On a human face, I reflected, such protuberances would have seemed like some dreadful disease. One of them looked like a little white mouse trying to get out. I covered up these phenomena again and left them to it, wondering what they would do next.

After a few weeks I again visited this earthly laboratory to see how things were getting on. I found that the protuberances had become much longer and had curled round at their ends—now white snakes coming out of the humble solid. They had curly heads like purplish knots, and some of these knots had half opened into a series of green ears. And now there was another addition: at the place where these stems, as we may now call them, came out of the potato, a network had been set up, of string, as it were, connecting the outfit with the soil. These, the roots, went downwards seeking the darkness of the earth, while every stem rose up to seek the light. But as yet there was no indication where or how new potatoes could appear.

During these early weeks the surface of the field showed no sign that anything was going on underneath. Later the whole brown surface began to change into rows of green—the light-seeking stalks had risen into the air and unfurled their leaves. As the weeks passed, and the months, these little green bushes grew in size and complexity until in late July they were all flowering—and a very pretty field it then looked. As all flowers have fruit, so had these—potato fruits, of course. But not the ones we eat.

Even after the green rows had appeared above-board and I made a further examination below I still did not see where the crop of potatoes was going to come from. Eventually the problem cleared itself up. I found them forming at the end of the network of roots. A few of the roots began to swell at their extremity—first about the size of a bird's egg, then a baby's shoe, getting larger and larger until some of them were four times the size of the original potato planted in the ground. And here we come to the curious thing about potatoes. The substance which grows at the end of the root is not itself a root. It is a *branch*. It is not a root, the botanists say, because roots do not bear buds and do not bear leaves, while this, the potato, does have buds and does have leaves (in the shape of scales). It is a subterranean branch, swollen and misshapen, storing up food for its buds; and botanists, no longer having the courage to call it a branch, call it a tuber. So when we plant a potato we are not planting a seed, we are not planting a root; we are planting a branch from whose gateways, called 'eyes', roots reach down and stalks reach up.

To complete the circle, what happens to the original potato? It conforms to the rule of eternal return by virtue of which the invisible becomes visible, and the visible takes on invisibility. It darkens, it softens, it becomes a squashy brown mash, and finally is seen no more. I used to enjoy taking it up in my hand when I saw it lying on the ground looking like an old leather purse. It had performed a remarkable act. Now its work was done. All the virtue had gone out of it. It had given its life to the green stalks above and the tubers below. Here I seemed to see a familiar sight in nature; many things coming from one thing, much from little, even something out of nothing. This is what we seem to see. Yet it is not so. True, the original potato started the business going, sending down those roots and sending up those stalks; but they in their turn built the building. The earth is not a solid; it is chiefly gas. The air is not thin; it is massed with food. Those roots sucked gases from the earth, those leaves sucked gases from the sky, and the result was the visible, hard, concrete potato. When we eat a potato we eat the earth, and we eat the sky. It is the law of nature that all things are all things. That which does not appear to exist to-day is to-morrow hewn down and cast into the oven. Nature carries on by taking in her own washing. That is Nature's economy, contrary to political economy; so that he who cries 'Wolf! Wolf!' is numbered amongst the infidels. 'A mouse,' said Walt Whitman, 'is enough to stagger sextillions of infidels.' Or a potato. What is an infidel? One who lacks faith. What creates faith? A miracle. How then can there be a faithless man found in the world? Because many men have cut off the nervous communication between the eye and the brain. In the madness of blindness they are at the mercy of intellectual nay-sayers, theorists, theologians, and other enemies of God. But it doesn't matter; in spite of them, faith is reborn whenever anyone chooses to take a good look at anything—even a potato.

2. THE WORM

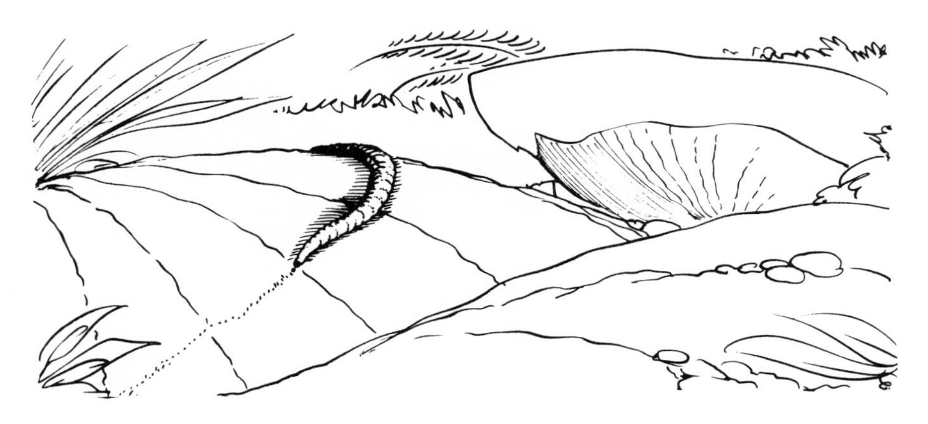

I HAVE heard it said more than once that the reason why there are now more wire-worms afflicting the crops than in the past is because there are more tractors. The idea being that since the tractor-driven plough turns over three or four furrows at a time as against the horse-plough's one furrow, the result is that the birds get far fewer troughs in which to find worms. Thus more worms are left in the soil.

It is an attractive theory. There is something cheering in the knowledge that Nature always hits back. It is metaphysically inspiring, if physically discouraging. Everything in nature has a meaning and a purpose. Everything is necessary to the universal scheme, every germ, every microbe, every pest. When anything ceases to serve the harmony it dies out. When man threatens the harmony he is attacked in one way or another. Those who dislike the advent of tractors see the multiplication of the wire-worm as an example of Nature's revenge.

Unfortunately there is a difficulty about this latter case. We cannot suppose that the seagulls and other birds who eat the worms are always agriculturally-minded. We cannot count on their patriotism in eating only wire-worms and leaving all the earth-worms. And if wire-worms do harm to the soil, earth-worms do a great deal of good. In so far as the birds have less chance to eat them we could argue with equal plausibility that the soil thereby gains by the tractor.

Eyeless, legless, faceless, earless, voiceless, the earth-worm is not much to look at—a mere squirming piece of flesh. Yet with its powerful muscles, its two stomachs (one inside and one outside), and its false teeth, it is able to carry out remarkable works.

These worms are the only creatures that eat the earth. They eat clay. They do not digest it neat like a piece of chocolate. As it passes through they extract from it organic matter in the shape of ova, larvae, spores of cryptogamic plants, and micrococci. That is the first reason why they swallow earth. They swallow it also in order to make their underground passages, their burrows—casting the material upwards into delicate little towers. This continuous mining has prodigious results. Charles Darwin estimated that fifty thousand worms often inhabit an acre of ground, and subsequent counts have put the figure at a million or more in rich soil. Since each worm ejects from twelve to twenty ounces a year, we find that from seven to eighteen tons of earth are frequently thrown up every year on an acre. Thus stones lying about on an uncultivated field will sink at the rate of two inches a year, so that in thirty years you can gallop a horse over what was once stony ground without its hoofs striking a single stone. Sometimes there are so many worms at work that a narrow stone path across a lawn will sink so quickly that a gardener cannot control it. Some of the slabs of Stonehenge have already gone down a good way, though it will take time before the rest of the ruins disappear from sight.

The worm is a friend to archaeologists who owe to it the preservation of many ancient objects. Coins, gold ornaments, stone implements are buried and stored for future inspection. Not long ago a neglected field near Shrewsbury which was ploughed-up revealed arrow-heads used at the Battle of Shrewsbury. The war-time ploughing-up has brought to light many new objects—a bomb which fell near my neighbour's house blew a Roman knife into his bedroom window. But that is only the minor museum-work of worms: villas, abbeys, pavements, walls, even towns have been carefully preserved by them. The remains of a large Roman villa at Chedworth, found under a wood by a gamekeeper digging for rabbits in 1877, with coins lying about dated A.D. 350; the tessellated pavement of Beaulieu Abbey; eighteen chambers of a Roman house at Brading in the Isle of Wight, with coins dated A.D. 337; the walls, tesserae, pottery, and coins of Roman Emperors from A.D. 133 to 361 dug up at Abinger marking another villa deserted fifteen hundred years ago; the town of Silchester with a wall eighteen feet high extending a mile and a half round a space of a hundred acres—all these, according to established authority, had been let down into the earth by the action of worms.

Another by-product of their activities consists in lowering the hills and widening the valleys of the land. Wherever there is a tumulus, an embankment, a hill, a slope, a valley which is not made of gravel or pure sand, worm castings will be thrown up, and then through the action of rain and wind their towers of earth will roll to the bottom so that gradually the mound is lessened. Small effects have vast results in the calendar of nature, and the eye that could keep watch across the passage of centuries might see the Sussex Downs and the Dorset slopes vanishing through the movement of worms.

Their general work is more ambitious. They create soil. Everyone knows that rock is really solid soil. When it becomes broken up and mixed with vegetable ash it is called clay. Worms, by means of acids and salts which they digestively generate, carry out a steady decomposition of rock. They go further; they wear down the small particles of rock which other agencies can do little to diminish, by grinding them in their gizzards with beads of glass and angular fragments of bricks or tiles which they employ as millstones or artificial teeth in order to crush the earth that they so largely consume. At the same time they add to the organic matter in the soil by the astonishing number of half-decayed leaves which they draw into their burrows to a depth of two or three inches. These leaves are moistened, torn into shreds, partially digested, and intimately mingled with earth—thus giving vegetable mould its uniform dark tint. This mould differs from subsoil by the absence of fragments and particles of stone which are larger than a worm can swallow.

It is pleasant to reflect when we look out upon an expanse of land with a fine superficial mould that it has all been swallowed by worms, that it has all passed and will pass again through the bodies of worms. For during the course of this journey the finer particles are sifted from the coarser, the whole mixed with vegetable debris, and saturated with intestinal secretions, so that the ground is prepared as by a gardener for the growth of fibrous-rooted plants and seedlings of all sorts. The soil is turned over and over, it is in perpetual motion. Thus the worms plough, and thus they harrow. They drain the land also; their burrows which often penetrate to a depth of five or six feet provide a vast drainage system. And yet another thing: they make way for aerial penetration, and they greatly facilitate the downward passage of moderate roots. They go further: they specially nourish those roots with the humus that lines their burrows like a cemented tunnel.

It would seem that before we proclaim that it is a bad thing for tractors to aid the preservation of wire-worms, we should consider whether it is not a good thing that they should aid the preservation of earth-worms. But it is possible that some people are uninstructed concerning this monarch among animals. I have not observed golfers flinch at the spectacle of thousands of dead worms on the fairway poisoned for their pleasure. Some people know nothing of the worm save that it 'will turn' under certain unspecified circumstances. Others, when they have cut one in half, honestly feel that they have performed an act of creation, making two creatures proceed where there had been only one before. There are no songs in its name. True, the poet who bent the most concentrated gaze upon the tiger, and saw that in it the fire of life burned brightest, was also he who, looking down into the damp, dark earth, perceived the worm and said—'Art thou a worm? Image of weakness, art thou but a worm? I see thee like an Infant wrappèd in the Lily's leaf.' Yet even he may not have known that the worm is more powerful than the tiger, that by its vast operations in ploughing, in harrowing, in levelling, in draining, in airing, in manuring, and even in creating soil, it adds to the wealth of nations and governs the destiny of man; and that given time and condition it could remove a mountain and cause a city to vanish from the face of the earth.

3. CONTEMPLATION UPON ANTS

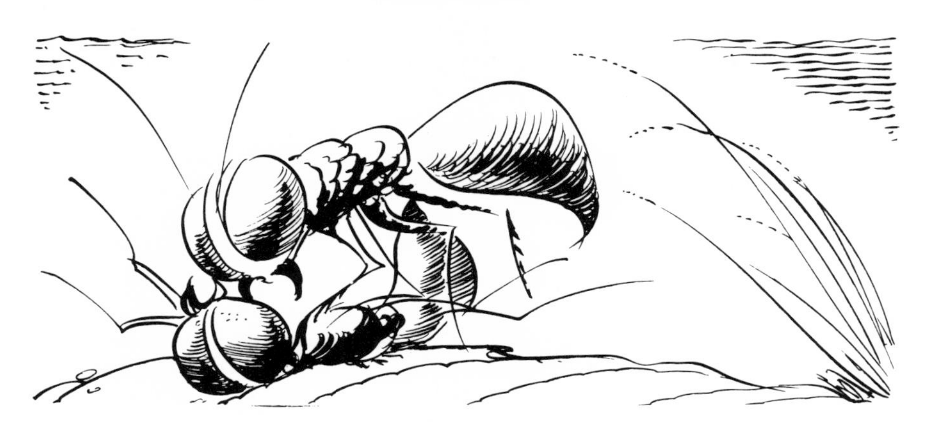

I TOOK a horse and cart and a good sharp spade and went across to a field that had to be ploughed up. It had been neglected for many years and now contained a large number of ant-hills. To promote easier ploughing the removal of these hillocks was necessary, and this was my task. My method was simple: first a hard blow downwards with the perpendicular blade through the centre of the mound; then a similar thrust at right angles across that cut; after which a few digs at the base enabled me to take out large slices and throw them on to the cart. When it was full I drove it away and dumped the lot into a pit. It took me some weeks, working all day, before I had cleared that field of ants.

And the odd thing is that I can say this, I can write it down here, and it will be accepted by the reader as a perfectly ordinary proceeding, a normal and rather tedious piece of agricultural work. That is all it is, provided we do not pause to think. I do not advocate that we should thus pause: for how could Man face reality, the reality of what he daily does, and yet pursue his way? When I did pause, sometimes, to consider what I was doing on that field I could not fail to feel the enormity of my act. The shining blade crashed down through the centre of a city built up with skill and labour; the inhabitants were thrown into confusion; then another flash and crash of the blade, and another, till bits of the home were flying through the air—thus my work for hour after hour and day after day.

Sometimes I stooped down to watch the effect of this spade-work, and saw the ants hurrying about desperately in every direction, most of them carrying white parcels considerably larger than themselves, going a little way in one direction then turning back at an obstruction and trying another route. Then my spade got to work again, sometimes neatly taking up a whole hill and chucking it into the cart. My power of destruction over this ant-world was really prodigious, as if a giant with legs the height of Snowdon and arms as long as the Sussex Downs, were to throw London away in an hour or so. I wondered whether even the ant-specialists (whom I now began to study) could really imagine just how these ants would begin to restore order upon the heterogeneous conglomeration into which their planned cities had been thrown.

Mankind has often been depressed and sometimes alarmed by ants. Schopenhauer, never notable for excessive cheerfulness, was much pained by contemplation of the Australian bull-dog ant. For if it is cut in two it fights with itself, a battle begins between the head and the tail. The head seizes the tail with its teeth, and the tail defends itself ferociously by stinging the head. Such battles have been known to last for half an hour, until the combatants died or were dragged away by other ants, themselves perhaps appalled by the spectacle. Still, Schopenhauer might have been cheered by the thought that at any rate here pain, as we know it, was absent, just as it was surely absent in that spider reported by Forel to have made a meal of its own leg amputated by itself, and in those caterpillars who occasionally devour their own tails.

Yet a creature like that Australian ant which can be increased by division is phenomenal, since animals differ from plants precisely in the fact that when you divide plants you multiply them, but when you divide animals you destroy them. That bull-dog ant was behaving like a curious kind of plant; but of course its double life was as brief as it was brutal. It is true that the head of an ant does not represent its capital in the same way as our heads do, and that decapitation need not always imply death. Dr. C. P. Haskins mentions an ant which carried on a fairly normal life for forty days without its head, but he does not suggest that this was a good thing for it, or that such a mode could be encouraged and developed. In a battle, a complete ant may be seen engaged in combat with a number of still ferocious heads, but those heads have no future.

An average specimen of the species, when it has all its limbs intact, presents a formidable design. What it lacks in beauty it gains in function. When we contemplate its two stomachs, one social and the other personal; its sting and poison bag; its four pumps; its brush and comb; its teeth that serve in turn as a battle axe, a pair of shears, a flour mill, and even a leg; its two elongated and movable noses with which it speaks, and with which it sees the shapes of things, and which serve it as a compass when far from home—we feel that personal functionalism could go no further. Yet its individual equipment is enhanced by its resource in composition; for not only can a single ant become a bottle, a door or a carriage when necessary, but a company of ants can turn themselves into a boat, a bridge, a tent, a ladder, a tunnel, or a covered road according to the needs of the hour.

The strength of their muscles in proportion to their size is such that we must compare it with that of a man who could easily lift his motor car over a fence, while their speed at getting about should be compared with a man going at twenty-five miles an hour on foot. Their endurance is so great that some can live without food for three months. They can do without air for a week, or if drowned, come to life again. Their energy seems indefatigable. This very morning, one having arrived on my book and run across it, I turned the book round so that it ran up again. I kept turning it round every time the ant reached the end. It never paused for breath. A long time passed and still I turned my book presenting it with an everlasting hill, and still it ran at a tremendous rate without need of rest or fuel, and making no distinction between the flat and perpendicular. In the end I grew weary of my role and anxious at its anxiety.

This Form in which life has been able to express itself, has been found so suitable—or so necessary to the economy of the world—that there are now over three thousand five hundred different species of ants, none of which can inter-breed. Their history is of immense length, disappearing into the misty millions of years that preceded the arrival of man. Thus by now their variations are many and extreme; especially in terms of size, for in this matter they differ so monstrously that some are a thousand times larger than others living in the same nest, the difference being truly as great as if one kind of man could walk about in the palm of another man's hand, or climb the Everest of his brow. Their adaptability and their expeditionary zeal are so pronounced that they can be found everywhere (except in Iceland, for some strange unreason). In regions of perpetual snow; in the burning sands of the desert; on the loneliest islands of the ocean; in the thick of the massive vegetation of jungles; on ships sailing in every direction—wherever we choose to look, there we shall find colonies of ants adapting themselves to their circumstance, displaying bright colours in warm climates, black and grey in cold countries, and discarding their eyes when, like the *Stigmatomma*, they live wholly beneath the soil in coniferous forests or seek to set up their galleries in the fastnesses beneath mighty rocks. The celerity and thoroughness of their movement in colonial expansion finds the best exemplar in the *Iridomyrmex* which in fifty years had spread from Argentina to England, and from England to Asia.

The number of the different species is immense, but of course some lines are more famous than others, commanding the astonishment and sometimes the fear of their human spectators. We thing of the terrible carnivorous Siafu ants who, though blind, nose their way on vast expeditions, attacking any creature they come across, large or small, with insatiable savagery and blind impassioned gluttony. All living creatures, including man, fly before the holocaust of their locust-like tempestuous plague. Fowls, horses, and donkeys are dispatched by them in a single night; the skeletons of mules and monkeys, of parrots, rats, and mice are left in their wake; the largest serpent in Africa does not escape them; while at Tanga it is said that the natives found them killing a leopard. We think of the Legionary Ants, the nomads who find no rest, doomed for ever to scurry in long marching columns across the forest floors in search of flesh and blood, never able to stay and colonize but condemned to march onward in unappeasable hunger. These are they who bivouack in tents composed of their own living bodies, who conduct their nymphs through roads arched by themselves when the sun is too hot, who again use their bodies in the composition of a bridge when they come to streams, and who, rolling themselves into a compact ball, float down rivers to new destinations.

These have been called the Visiting Ants, and they are fighters. But many more of the species fight, and indeed carry on wars in a deliberate scientific manner. These wars have engaged the notice of mankind perhaps more than any other of their activities, for on this subject we are glad to find other species as bad as ourselves. And it is true that war, as opposed to jungle-fighting, is the correct word. For it is cold-blooded and planned. They do not fight for the immediate satisfaction of hunger, but for theft. One species will attack the fortress of another with the sole object of carrying off the larvae for future food or slaves. Thus the militant *Polyesgus* captures every year forty thousand cocoons from the *Fusca* or the *Rufibarbis*, while one Amazon colony has been known to carry out forty-four raiding expeditions in the course of a month. The manoeuvres are real military operations, squadrons and cohorts deployed in strategic formations carrying out concerted movements of attack bearing an extraordinary resemblance to the warfare of mankind. Unlike men, they are their own weapons. Just as they grow tools upon their bodies for civil life so they are their own sabres and their own flame-throwers. A quick thrust from the battle-axed mandible of a soldier-ant and the head of another is pierced to the brain. An enlarged picture of an ant squirting its poison-jet at the advancing foe is almost an illustration of the terrible flame-throwers that scattered the Germans in 1944 (a weapon so ghastly in conception no less than execution that we pretended not to know about it). Battles between ants provide many strange scenes. It is then that we can see a giant ant overcome by a company of small ones running along its legs, climbing upon its head, and sawing off its limbs. Then we may witness a victorious ant, minus a few limbs, with the severed heads of its attackers still biting, and fastened upon it like the gargoyles on a cathedral. We may even see the heads of two enemies, after decapitation, carrying on the combat. The fury of some of their battles has been known to continue without cessation for as long as a month and a half.

We pass, and we pass willingly, from these scenes to the contemplation of their peaceful pursuits. They live in what might almost be called cities. The nests in the shape of little hills such as I have been digging out and carting away, provide but one example of their architecture. They make them in earth in Europe, on trees in forests, in sand in the desert; they may raise them dome-shaped or dig below the surface making a crater or rampart above; they build round the stems of grass so that the stalks make a pillared hall of many compartments; they get beneath stones, employing the slab as a ready-made dome; they use marshes and peat bogs, the crevices of rocks, the cavities of certain tropical leaves, the caves of oak-galls, even the perpendicular tunnels of dry stalks; they sculpture their homes out of the trunks of rotten trees and beneath the barks of sound ones; they find room for their communities in the beams of houses, chalets, and bridges, sometimes causing them to fall; they make carton nests by using their glandular secretions to consolidate wood-rot, sand, or fungus; they cultivate gardens in the forks of trees, planting the epiphytes of the genus *Cordin*, the resultant roots giving them the framework for their arboreal habitations; and many of the nests to be seen upon the trees by the astonished traveller in Eastern lands are made of leaves and the finest silk woven by means of the thread of their own larvae which serve as shuttles.

Equally various is the interior arrangement of galleries, corridors, storerooms, nurseries, and dormitories. Here, then, they live their lives, many hundreds of them together on the basis of mutual service. In short, they are societies. That is how we see them: as individuals working together deliberately for the good of all. But *they* do not see it like that. They do not see it at all. They have no conceptions. And if occasionally the glimmering of intelligence seems to inform their actions it is generally when they do something foolish and in vain. They are not held together as we are held together, by an economic nexus and by conscious motives. Invisible wires draw them together as if they were a whole giving an illusion of parts. We cannot fathom this. We may utter the word *instinct*, but can we understand, can we conceive life lived under the command and in the keeping of a directing force not consciously obeyed? Can we, even with a mighty effort, imagine living for a single day when nearly all our actions are *done for us* as some of our actions, notably the movements of our stomachs, are done for us without thought and without reprieve?

It is too difficult, and more profitable, to contemplate their economy and exchange. Their distribution of labour is based upon a scheme of bodily structure. They act according to their speciality. The females can lay eggs and rear their young; the males can fertilize the females, after which they cast themselves aside, now useless, and therefore unworthy to live. The remainder, wingless workers, carry on according to the tools they display. Thus he who has a jaw like a battle-axe will act as soldier; he who has mandibles like clippers will cut leaves; he who has grain-grinding jaws will serve as miller and make flour; he who has a head like a wall will live the life of a door; he who has a head like a bucket will be a wheelbarrow; and, above all, he who has a good communal stomach will be a barrel. This last has been celebrated by all myrmecologists. In order to be prepared against barren days when food is scarce, a considerable number of worker-ants suffer their social stomachs to be filled with a great amount of liquid food until they swell so much as to look like barrels with a few handles in the shape of claws. These sacks of skin are hung in rows along the ceilings of the storerooms in the nest; and there they can be seen, living honey-jars, ant-bottles, awaiting the day when they shall be tapped for the benefit of the community. They are never thrown away as empties, but are continually refilled by their fellows. They remain where they are; that is their life now, they know no other; they hang from the roof until they die. This is intolerable! we say. It must be torture, such an existence. They can have no feelings, they can have no thoughts. They cannot really be individuals, for no separate being could be capable of so total an obedience or so great a sacrifice.

Thus ants are specialized in activity, but they all share common destinies and dooms. All, for instance, are without ears, and live in a world dedicated to silence. Here again we cannot easily conceive this life. There is silence along their streets, and even on the field of battle there is no sound. And since they are deaf it seems certain that they are also voiceless. It may be that we have not the ears to hear the utterances of insects even as we have not the eyes to see the tiniest of their brothers. Anyway the fact is that we don't hear anything and it is probable that the silence is absolute. Just as we can watch a spider attack a fly caught in its web and see it slowly eat its living meal without a sound being heard, so also, however close we might bend down upon cohorts of embattled ants, we will hear no shout of insectual command, no cry of triumph, no moans of the dying, and even when a head is sawn off or a severed limb falls to the ground, no shriek of pain will humanize the scene.

Ants also share the possession of remarkable antennae. Their sensitivity to smell is perhaps their salient characteristic. They are able to detect objects from a long way off by their antennae, which can best be described as extended noses. These serve the ants as a far more reliable guide for finding their way about than their eyes, when they have any. By smell alone they are able to sense the *shape* of things—which is as good as seeing them. And since they are movable, the ants can use them for other purposes as well. They can wave them as flags, thus signalling directions to each other. They can apply them as whips to urge sluggards to action or awaken them to danger. Most important, these antennae are their chief means of speech. They hold antennal conversation, expressing their feelings, their discoveries, their anxieties, and their intentions with the aid of signs which they read as easily as we read the book or the tongue.

Each species of ant has a different smell and thus the formicaries are consolidated by a brotherhood of smell. By this means one species is able to spot the vicinity of another species that will supply them with slaves. For though ants support each other in their nests and formicaries on the basis of mutual exchange even to the extent of feeding one another by process of regurgitation, they raid other species for extra labour. Foremost amongst these are the Amazon Ants who advance in strategic formation upon a suitable alien fortress in order to carry away the larvae and subsequently train up this progeny. Larvae are used by ants as a form of food. They often eat their own larvae. But since this practice is as unsatisfactory for them as it would be for hens to live on their own eggs, they seek to procure the larvae of other species. Thus there is an evolution here from food to slavery. Certain ants began by raiding other nests for larvae as food. But sometimes they didn't eat them all and the larvae hatched out and grew into workers perfectly ready to serve their masters, since naturally they were unaware that those 'parents' were really masters and they were slaves. The process continued until gradually the habit of procuring larvae for slaves as well as for food became established. This developed until the slave workers did practically everything for their owners who at last could not even eat without assistance, and if neglected, starved in the midst of plenty: for here, as elsewhere, we see the end of all slavery, which is the turning of the tables, the revolution of the wheel, when the masters become slaves and the slaves masters.

In fact the host becomes parasitic upon the guest. But there are also a number of genuine parasites who are tolerated by their hosts. One of the most pleasing characteristics of ants is their cleanliness, and to this end they grow upon their bodies a brush and comb. But they can have their ablutions thoroughly attended to by certain parasites who like nothing better than to lick them for hours: hence we find a large species such as the *Myrmica* suffering the attentions of a small species, the *Leptothorax*, who ride about upon them and perpetually lick them, receiving in turn abundance of food. The parasites by no means always belong to the species of ant. In all, three thousand species of insects are harboured by ants for reasons clear or obscure. The most familiar to us are the aphids, the leaf-hoppers, and other sap sucking insects who are kept for the sweet secretions which they exude. In fact they are domesticated animals like cows, and the ants keep them apart in stables to promote regular milking. The secretions of the parasite-beetles, the *Lomechusa*, are particularly popular amongst ants, but we can hardly speak of these beetles in terms of cattle because their hosts regard the delicacy which they receive from them with such favour that they look after and bring up the beetle-grubs with greater care than their own offspring—even allowing them to eat the ant-grubs!

When we think of ants we generally visualize extreme order and efficiency, but the oddity of the parasitic intrusion undermines this idea. If we ourselves were to sit down to table with porcupines, alligators and lobsters, and to feed them at the expense of our own children; if we were indifferent to crickets nearly as large as ourselves; if our houses were inhabited, against our wills, by cockroaches the size of wolves, and flies the size of hens; if we fed monstrous animals with our babies because they exuded whisky, we could hardly stress the efficient ordering of our lives. Yet that is a fair comparison, according to Wheeler and Huxley, with the habits of ants. Moreover, there are many parasites who climb, creep, and intrude into the fold on false pretences, and by virtue of mimicry deceive their hosts with all the cunning of certified hysterical swindlers. These are often beetles who slip about undetected, ready to devour the helpless, to steal from the unwary, or to ride upon ants while sucking their blood. Some specialize at intercepting the morsel of food in its passage from one ant to another at the moment of regurgitation—a disappearing trick which bewilders the authors of this amiable practice. The highly individual tricks of the *Clythra* command our respect; this is a small beetle who builds itself into a little barrel of damp earth and walks about in this condition on its front legs. On the approach of an ant it stops and draws its legs under the barrel, thus presenting the ant with a convenient place in which to lay eggs: and when the eggs are deposited the little truck moves on, and the *Clythra* enjoys a good meal. More sinister is the species *Phorid* who attacks a big worker of the large *Camponotus pennsylvanicus* until it has succeeded in laying an egg in its neck between the head and the pronotum. This is the ant's death sentence, because once the egg is laid the subsequent larva creeps right into the head where it devours the muscles and brain, the ant meanwhile wandering about in a state of increasing stupefaction until at last, becoming motionless, it hangs down its ever emptying head. When everything possible has been eaten in this interior the parasite cuts the last ligaments that join the head to the body of the ant, which then falls to the ground, thus providing a safe and comfortable cocoon in which the larva can turn into a nymph. Not less grim in execution and more extraordinary in result is the action of the female parasite aptly called *Bothriomyrmex decapitans* who having got into a formicary, seeks out the queen, considerably larger than herself, mounts upon her back and spends a few days sawing off her head: and no sooner has the head dropped than the parasite is adopted by the community she has invaded and whose queen she has murdered.

It will be observed from all the foregoing that appetite and great hunger are salient characteristics of ants. We have noted some of the ways by which they satisfy their desires. But they are highly ingenious creatures, and besides feeding upon neotar, meat, and eggs they send out foraging parties to carry in grain from the harvests of mankind. Their nests contain elaborate cellars and storerooms underground, rather like those familiar shelters of our own which we must now number as the fourth necessity of Man. Here they store up their wheat grains, keeping them so dry that they seldom germinate—for actual grain-growing does not enter into their economy. Then the corn-grinding ants, with the special jaws, get to work and mash up the grain to a paste which hardens into little loaves of bread. (Forel speaks of ant-butchers also who prepare joints.) So considerable is this agricultural activity, so far-reaching the carrying of harvests, that their granaries have become the cause of litigation amongst farmers, and the object of certain clauses in the Talmudic Rules of the Jews. Even so we can hardly call these harvesting ants actual agriculturalists; but it would be a most proper term to apply to the Attiine ants who grow vegetables and live on them entirely. They cultivate a species of fungus with such continuity that it has become extinct in the wild state no less than the grasses cultivated by mankind. These ants, who sometimes have nests the size of cottages, reserve deep galleries for their fungus gardens which they not only keep clear of any sort of weed by assiduous *hoeing*, but send out the workers who possess leaf-cutting mandibles to bring in leaves, which they then chew into a compost for the fungi, as if in conformity with the requirements of Sir Albert Howard. Elaborate columns of these leaf-clippers leave the formicary, ascend trees in a body, cut down the leaves, and return home with them. 'It is an experience never to be forgotten,' says Dr. C. P. Haskins, 'when, returning tired and hungry through the misty jungle at eventide, one first stumbles across the foraging columns of the parasol ants, their course marked by a line of waving banners, vivid green against the rain-soaked earth, as they return laden homeward.'

Thus the ants live. Thus they work and eat and fight and forage, sometimes unbending in relaxation to indulge in mimic warfare, gymnastic jousting, or caterpillar-riding. But for the most part there is little time for these relaxations, and they attend without pause at the great task of eating to live and bringing up their young. The workers are as tireless inside the nest as outside, carrying out, with unfailing obedience to the forces that govern them, the complicated business of midwifery when they liberate the nymphs from their silken shrouds and usher them into the world. These neutralized workers are wingless and work for the present; but new formicaries must be established, more eggs laid, and foundations placed for the continuance of their ancient line. This is the task of the males and females. At a given hour, in a given locality, when the temperature is just right, there is a great stir amongst all the nests of a locality. The ants assemble outside their nests, male, female, and workers. The males and females spread their wings in the midst of the now excited assembly of workers and fly away, and even as they fly they perform the act of fertilization, the females sometimes carrying upon their backs three or four males who in turn are granted their brief instant of pleasure which is also their sentence of death. Their work is done and they must die: and the real work of the female begins. She descends to the earth and there burrows or seeks out a hole which shall serve as the beginnings of a new nest. In the darkness of her chamber she *takes off* her wings and throws them down into the earth, and by the aid of her salivary ducts converts them into a fatty substance which alone serves as food for the nourishment of her first brood. She herself either eats nothing or eats some of her own eggs; then lays some more, then eats some more, then lays some more. If she belongs to the genus *Atta* she will carry with her on her nuptial flight, in a special pocket, the hyphae of the fungi to which she is accustomed. She will deposit them in her chamber when they will speedily flourish under her care, receiving manure in the form of larvae and wings, after

which the mushrooms can be eaten by this queen and her daughters. And there we will leave her, brooding: a strange sight; nothing stranger than this in nature, a creature whose young are fed and whose fungi are nourished by virtue of her own body and her own eggs—a little circle within the great Circle of Life.

When instructed, I still remove ant-hills, throwing them in pieces on to a cart, in order that men may have fields to themselves. But as I raise the spade in spoliation of their temples I must let my mind play with humility upon the scenes of these lowly children of the earth. For it is the destiny of man that he should seek to take upon himself the burden of understanding, and to move in the comprehension of his works and the consciousness of his crimes. I gaze down upon these ants. I have looked into their houses, and passed along their ways, and sat beside their cradles—and yet I destroy them still! I do not know how much I really care about them; and am I not also fatally bound and driven by the laws of life, my brain and my heart as yet but tiny lanterns in the windy darkness of the world?

I give them my attention. I pass in review the singularity of their works. I sing their long and venerable history and rehearse the resourcefulness of their economy no less than the architectural versatility of their designs; and I would apologize to them if I could. But what I cannot do is to join with Solomon and say—Go to the ant. That was an unfortunate remark. To compare men with ants, as if there was significance in the comparison, is ridiculous. In its context, Solomon's remark may not have been so foolish as it sounds. Perhaps he was observing the tireless labouring of the harvesting ants over against the slackness of his own people, and in a moment of exuberance, said—Go to the ant, thou sluggard. After which, for generations to come, this supreme absurdity was canonized by the repetitions of unthinking publicists. For the wisdom of the wise is continually turned into the folly of the fool.

In saying this I would not wish it to be thought that all who have played with the idea are fools, least of all the great Forel, who, being very concerned about the League of Nations, could not refrain from using the ant to further that cause. But these loose comparisons will not do, and in the most recent book about ants (1946) they have reached an altitude of silliness beyond which other specialists will probably not easily ascend; a book wherein the regurgitation of ants is compared to an author writing books, their nests to the city of Athens, and the parasitic success of interlopers to the Chinese introduction of Buddhism among the people of Inner Mongolia. We may smile; but the general idea is equally absurd. There are similarities between the ways of ants and of men; comparisons can be made; but they should only be given a passing glance or as a joking reference.

There are many ants and there are many men—we can't get much out of that, especially as there are thousands of species of ants and only one of men. Ants live together and so do men, but many other animals live in nests and flocks and family groups, while the tight societies of ants bear no resemblance to the vast interconnections of men. Ants go in for a species of agriculture—but how silly to make a serious comparison with men. Ants wage war; and there you can truly make your comparison—but what of it? We may note with interest that slavery turns out as badly for them as for us. They keep domestic animals but are not quite so much their slaves as we are to ours, calling some of our own species not men, but *cow*-men. My point is that we can make comparisons for fun, and make jokes about them if we choose, but that is all. We cannot learn from them, nor be forewarned by them. Our ways are not their ways, neither is our destination theirs. Between us and the animals there is a great gulf fixed. The most important thing about man is that he is *not* an animal. He is different, and in this difference lies his ultimate hope and promise. A miracle happened to man when he was an animal. That miracle was the *birth of language.* This has made his life incomparable with any animal. We are not concerned merely with the difference *to* him which this miraculous event has made in the ordering of his life. It is the difference *in* him that is crucial. For this was the sign of the birth of consciousness. Not of intelligence, but of consciousness. Something *broke in* on man. It may have evolved, but it is not strictly a question of evolution. It is something outside evolution. Something to which the animals are not evolving. Life goes on, evolution goes on, but never does there come a time when any animal attains the miracle of language (which is not the same as capacity to communicate). Animals can do all sorts of things and become subdued to us in a hundred ways, but this obstinate difference remains. It does not matter how 'human' a dog is, how much it feels or understands, how dear it is to us; dogs can go on changing and evolving, but never will there come a time when they will be *spectators* and attain consciousness and use the instrument of consciousness, speech: no matter how extraordinary may be the tricks of a dog, we can never convey a Thought, as a thought, to it, never see it evolve to the point of our being able to say—'I'll be back on Sunday night.' Consciousness is the miracle of man. That is his whole significance, and the meaning of his imperfection, and his promise. Because it has broken in, because he does possess it, then it will evolve in him as it has already done, it will go on evolving; this burden of apartness and semi-understanding which he often feels too heavy to bear, will be lifted; he will attain a higher state of consciousness and enter again into the unity that he has lost. He should not turn to the animals for directions. He should not go to the ant. He should fix his gaze steadily upon this human gift that makes him unique, and see in it, and the evolution of it, the key to all his set-backs and the meaning of all his suffering.

4. WHILE STANDING ON A DUNGHILL

Good farmyard manure. I take large spadefuls of the stuff, like great slabs of chocolate cake, and throw them into a cart. As we open up the dunghill it begins to steam and its excellent odour becomes somewhat stronger. Various insects alight upon it. I cannot see the very small ones, of course, but would like to know the full insectitude activity. I observe one that always seems to be sharpening his forceps like a man in front of a joint—he of the brown wings. Also he of the beaked and vampire face. He of the dumb-bell body. He of the sleek and jet-black mail. I lift up their mountain of food into the cart, drive it off, and then throw it on the field. After which I climb on to another huge dunghill and fill up the cart again. And I must say I never felt better employed.

Not long ago the subject of manure and dunghills was regarded as low. There has been a great change. To-day it is considered almost a test of a man's intelligence how much he appreciates manure. Throughout the land, people who formerly thought it only proper to show off their herbaceous borders now call in their neighbours to admire their compost heaps. A housewife gathering up the droppings from the milkman's horse in the suburbs is a normal sight. Nearly everyone has already grasped that there is no such thing as *rubbish*. Some go so far as to declare, with Lord Northbourne, that a man who burns an old pair of trousers is committing murder.

Let me see if I can make farmyard manure slightly more intelligible to myself than hitherto. Where begin? It starts with the grass and the roots and the corn upon which stock feed. These things are burned in the furnaces of their stomachs. The ashes are passed out. Mixed with the straw of the stable they are piled up every day into a dunghill. As it stands it is no use. It would be strange if the grass having been eaten could then be immediately eaten again by grass. Yet this does occur after a time, and grass and other plants do eat this which has been already eaten. But it must first be treated. By whom? Not by man: he couldn't manage it. By whole empires of creatures visible only to the microscope, called bacteria. Though small they belong to the organic world and have their own special problems, not least of which is vigilance against gigantic enemies, also invisible to us, called protozoa who gobble them up.

These bacteria, minute and unhonoured, labour ceaselessly for the good of all mankind. Or, rather, of all life upon the earth. For without them not only would the manure-heap never be usable as food, but the soil itself would fail to serve, its chemicals would not co-ordinate, and the great sun itself would administer its blows of light in vain. Let their labour cease and all vegetation would be choked and the earth would become a wilderness, ugly and silent.

In order to carry out their great work they need above all things numbers; vast battalions of them must be on the job. Thus not the least interesting thing about them is their rate of birth. Within the compass of twenty-four hours one bacterium is capable of producing an offspring one hundred and seventy thousand times as numerous as the present population of the world. They multiply by division, and that division occurring every half hour, a single individual can become within the course of one day the ancestor of 280,000,000,000 bacteria. This is an adequate rate of birth, and therefore when we say that empires of them get to work on manure heaps and in the soil, we are making an understatement.

And what are the offices they perform? I confine myself to their work on the manure. In an ounce of soil there may be about 150,000,000 bacteria, but in a similar amount of manure there may be about 30,000,000,000. Broadly their labour consists in breaking down complex substances and in building up inert constituents into energetic bodies. Farmyard manure consists of excreta, urine, and the litter of the stable. The first movement in the bacterial symphony is the destruction of the litter and its conversion into a dark brown moist substance, humus, which finally retains none of the structure of the original straw. The manure proper contains a great variety of carbon compounds, with also phosphates and potash, which can be summed up as nitrogenous material, the nitrogen of which is not yet in a position to serve as food. So the next task of the bacteria is to bestow such order as may be necessary to release the vital potentials.

The hill heats. It is burning. It is shrinking. Could we watch what is happening we would perceive the waxing and waning of different armies of bacteria, each handling the material in turn. The first army seizes upon the nitrogen, tears it from its complex grouping, and splits off ammonia from its protein. We cannot see this operation, but we can smell it all right. That is the work of the first army; they then hand their product over to a second corps which immediately sets to work to change the ammonia into nitrate. This done the division of labour continues and a third army takes control turning the article finally into the soluble form of calcium nitrate.

Not that these operations always go through as smoothly as this. Too much oxygen may get in owing to a loosely piled hill, or unharmonious bacteria may undo the good work and de-nitrify the nitrate expelling it out in gases, until another body of bacteria comes forward, the gallant Azotobacters who, rising to the occasion, re-nitrify the de-nitrified and unburn the burnt—if I may be said to have followed the proceedings rightly.[1]

Anyway there is no place where I am more content to stand than here upon this dunghill, where that which is invisible is found to be mightier than the monumental mockeries of men—nay, where the things that are not, are raised above the things that are.

[1] See *Agricultural Bacteriology*, by John Percival. *Johnstone's Elements of Agricultural Chemistry*. *The Soil*, by F. H. King. *The Spirit of the Soil*, by G. D. Knox.

5. THE MYSTERY OF CLOUDS

WHILE harrowing one afternoon I saw a cloud looking like a cloud-capped tower itself. (I was pleased with it for this, for it did something to make up for the annoyance at having once seen a cloud like a grand-piano before ever I heard Trigorin report the same thing.) Then, as is my way, I asked myself, with resolute candour, how much I knew about clouds. Did I know what a cloud is? And as usual I found only a few bits and pieces of ill-related and undigested fact strewn about somewhere in the upper floor of my head. So, again according to practice, I threw the lot away and started from scratch.

First, as to the different kinds of cloud (for Nature seldom goes in for one sample of anything). They have been classified, of course, and named. It is amusing to read academic writers when they get going on the classification business. Studying such authorities one would really think that the clouds had been classified and named at the Beginning; whereas it is we who classify them in a frantic attempt to bestow order amongst them so that we may be able to see them better and grapple with them. Speaking for myself, however, I find that the exhaustive classification, including the inevitable sub-divisions to cover the numerous border cases, only makes the thing more mixed than ever, and I am content to acknowledge just three classes. First, the upper or Cirrus clouds often small and in vast droves of celestial sheep, wispy and frail—'flocks of Admetus under Apollo's keeping. Who else could shepherd such? He by day, dog Sirius by night; or huntress Diana herself—her bright arrows driving away the clouds of prey that would ravage her fair flocks'. They are often as high as thirty thousand feet and are not seen low. Second, the Rain clouds which are the lowest of all and are seen as wide films of grey and dark. Third, between these two lots there are seen accumulated heaps which are gathered under the general head of Cumulus. It is these last that hold our attention most.

What is a cloud? It is invisible water made visible. The atmosphere is full of water, but we cannot see it until too much of it gets up there. Then it suddenly becomes visible, like a magic flower growing out of nothing in the sky. The heat of the sun is constantly evaporating water from land and sea, and taking it up into the air until saturation point is reached—as declared by the clouds. I make that statement because it is 'authoritative' and I must be authoritative; but I do not understand it, since on that showing one might expect more clouds on a hot day than on a cold one. But let it pass.

Clouds are water, and they have weight—we know that much. Then why do they not sink to the ground? They should be continually falling at our feet. Yet they stay up there, though they are not supported from below nor held from above. These are simple questions; but the greatest descriptive writer of all time—he confined himself to the sea—acknowledged that he always found these simple problems 'the knottiest of all'. When I seek an answer to such questions to whom do I turn? Not to the schoolmasters, not to the academicians, not to the authorities. I turn always to the Masters, to the Stylists—to a Fabre, to a Melville, to a Ruskin. Is Ruskin puzzled by this? Of course. And his answer? He hasn't one. He says he can't make it out. 'I believe we do not know what makes clouds float. Clouds are water in some fine form or other: but water is heavier than air, and the finest form you can give a heavy thing will not make it float in a light thing. *On* it, yes; as a boat: but *in* it, no. Clouds are not boats, nor boat-shaped, and they float in the air, not on top of it.'

Yet perhaps the solution is provided in a book I have beside me on clouds by G. A. Clarke, F.R.P.S., F.R.MET.SOC. He does not raise this specific question deliberately or clearly, of course; but if I can pierce through the language in which such books are written, I think he says that clouds continually evaporate at the bottom and renew themselves at the top—so that our given cloud which should be falling at our feet does not do so because it is always ceasing to exist and always being rebuilt. But maybe he hasn't really said that, or wouldn't hold that he had said it—for the minor scientist, like the minor philosopher and the minor statesman, never likes to say anything definite.

Another question. How is it that clouds are so complete, so sharp in their outline? We look up into the sky and see these chiselled leviathans swimming through the ocean of air at the bottom of which we walk,

these drastic shapes each margined against the blue with a termination as clean as the Cliffs of Moher; but they are not solids, and the last thing we should expect is this firm binding of the unboundaried moisture in the airy wastes.

I turn again to Ruskin, and again he does not know the answer. 'What hews it into a heap, or spins it into a web?' he asks. 'Cold is usually shapeless, I suppose, extending over large spaces equally, or with gradual diminution. You can't have, in the open air, angles and wedges. and coils, and cliffs of cold. Yet the vapour stops suddenly, sharp and steep as a rock, or thrusts itself across the gates of heaven in likeness of a brazen bar; or braids itself in and out, and across and across, like a tissue of tapestry; or falls into ripples, like sand; or into waving shreds and tongues, as fire. On what anvils and wheels is the vapour pointed, twisted, hammered, whirled as the potter's clay? By what hands is the incense of the sea built up into domes of marble?'

No doubt there are up-to-date answers to such questions; but personally I would just as soon leave it there. Certainly there is nothing in Nature more mysterious than clouds. And nothing stirs the imagination more than those creatures that are not alive; those buildings not made of brick; those domed and daring palaces in which there reigns no king; those vast foundries flaming without fire; those mountain ranges upon which no feet may ever walk; those radiant prospects of a far country belonging to the paradise lost regions of the heart. They stir us; but they do not calm, they cannot soothe. 'We all look up into the blue sky for comfort,' said Coleridge, 'but nothing appears there, nothing comforts, nothing answers us, and so we die.' And if we see therein some clouds, vessels made of water, journeying to nowhere and appearing out of nothing, they do not answer us, they bring no comfort. Indeed we have to be strong in spirit to bear looking at them at all. We must not be depressed. We must not be ill. We must not be worried. We must not be in debt. We must not be in prison: there is real agony in Wilde's for ever haunting lines on the wistful look cast 'Upon that little tent of blue We prisoners called the sky, And at every careless cloud that passed In happy freedom by'. We must not be feeling futile—for then they will seem infuriatingly futile and drive us mad. It must not be Sunday afternoon in a town; we know what Franz Kafka meant when, feeling miserable on a Sunday afternoon, he was 'astonished sometimes by the almost unending senseless passing of the dull clouds'. It must not be in time of war. We cannot cloud-gaze to-day (1943). The time is not yet, but even as I write the time draws near when many who saw them only as the phantoms of their fears, shall hail them as the messengers of joy and peace.

6. THE BOOKS OF STONE

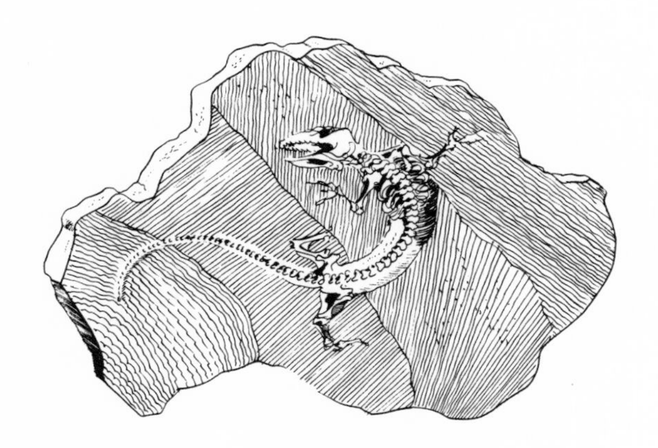

ONE day, while ploughing the chalky Dorset down, my share threw up many stones. When, at the headland, I stopped my horses and lifted the turn-furrow clear of the soil, I saw that a number of attractive-looking flints lay at my feet. I picked up a few of them. They were all much alike: flat on one side, and on the other shaped like a little hill; and upon that hill a graceful design was traced: a star with five wings, some deeply engraved—embanked railway-tracks with sleepers the size of ribs on a nail-file.

They were the flint-casts of sea-urchins belonging to the Chalk Age of the earth in the Mesozoic Era. One hundred million years ago those creatures had made their likeness, had traced their death-masks on the flowing flint. One hundred million years ago these very things I looked at were existing! Was it Time made visible? Did I hold Eternity in the palm of my hand? Standing there in that lonely and lovely place, on that bare ocean-moulded hill, in November 1944, I pressed my mind back through the bottomless abysses of time, back beyond the dawn of man, beyond the Tertiary, beyond the Eocene, back to the Cretacean shore.

Then Australia and New Zealand, joining with Africa and South America, made a single mass. The north of England and Ireland were one with America and with Norway. The Mediterranean flowed across the Sahara Desert. Italy lay buried in the deep. Some of France emerged, but Paris was the centre of a deep basin. Holland, Belgium, Denmark, and the regions of the Rhine were all part of a sea that stretched to the Carpathians. The south of England was submerged. Such is the general picture; but we are dealing with unmeasured immensities of time—this given period covering over fifty million years itself—and during that age the site of London alone, for instance, seems to have been above and below water several times. To-day we think of the long, wild washing of the Atlantic waves and of the depth of that water: it is hard indeed to think of it ever as land—still less of becoming land again, as may happen, when the enfossilled wrecks of ships will reveal their tale of violence and death. It is hard to think of an enthroned mountain peak or sheep-grazed valley as folded in the arms of the sea. Yet thus it has been. Many parts of the earth have been widely flooded, and then have risen again, only to sink once more. But the rate of rising and sinking, according to the measurements to be read from the rocks, is in the nature of one foot in ten thousand years. At the moment we might be pardoned for considering this stationary. But there are no stations upon earth: not one single thing is fixed; and though I may stand to-day upon the hill, deciphering the tablets of stone, I must learn that the cold waves flowed here before, smoothing out these rounded hills, and that they may flow again and wash away our chronicle. . . . Not quite, though; future fossils too will make their script, and the mighty Mind, exalted above all time, will read the pages of the flinty books.

Between the end of the Jurassic and the beginning of the Tertiary Era a great amount of chalk was formed. It was such a striking episode that the whole period has been called the Cretaceous Age. Minute and innumerable oceanic animals, called foraminifera, floating about near the surface of the sea, sunk to the bottom when dead, and then accumulated in a slowly solidifying ooze. We call the resultant accumulation Chalk. If we examine a handful of it under a microscope we find that it consists of the casing of the foraminifera—really shells of the most delicate and beautiful design, six thousand to a square inch. In view of the fact that such deposits are only found to-day at a depth of about twelve thousand feet, it would seem that this Dorset hill was once in the abysses of the sea whose surface flowed where the low flying clouds float now. . . . We approach the white cliffs of Dover, and gaze upward at the seeming solid shows of earth and rock. It is well to realize the reality, that this too is water or chiefly water in another style, and that upon the backs of innumerable urchins of the sea our history is stayed.

The era that is called Chalk is given a span of some sixty-five million years, and is said to have ended roughly one hundred million years ago—(though we can hardly suppose that foraminifera were absent from the seas in either Jurassic, Triassic, or Tertiary times). It is proper to call the Cretaceous Age modern if we are willing to think realistically of Time: for the earth had already rolled for two thousand million years.

We can call it modern, also, because some of the trees and flora familiar to-day began to appear. Man was not to arrive on earth for another hundred million years; and yet the scene would not seem wholly strange to us even now. Ferns, sedges, and reeds in marshes and swampy places; a grove of poplars against a winter's sky; willows and alders by a river bank; laurels, magnolias, and vines on the hillside; elms, oaks, conifers, maples, palms, and eucalyptus trees: all these things, so familiar to us, had ancestors rooted at that time. 'No man knows' said Walter de la Mare, 'Through what wild centuries Roves back the rose.' Flowering plants do reach back to the Cretacean lands, while the ancestry of trees breaks the boundaries of our conception. To this day we can see, on the shore of the Isle of Wight, a Chalk Age conifer which had been swept down a river and buried with silt, a twenty foot length of fossiled trunk, indifferent to the assault of centuries. The leafy arbour, the climbing ivy on the bended trunk, reel back in time beyond our power to pass in thought; that is why, seated in such a place on a summer's day, we lose ambition, and hardly claim identity, made languid by an air that joins us with the immeasurable wastes of the Mesozoic.

Some of the animals of that time are also familiar to us, and have sent representatives down to our day. Then, as now, the crocodile lay on the shore like a log of wood; that slippery rope of life we call the snake was there; the four-legged footstool of stone named turtle had his place. In those days they had the whole earth as their playground. But they did not rule it, they were not the lords of life. There were other creatures, more formidable, who have sent us no messengers. These were the Dinosaurs. They were the supreme beings of that world—though called by us monsters. They ruled throughout the Jurassic and lasted until the end of the Cretaceous Era. There were many of them—in Britain alone at least one hundred and twenty-one different kinds. They have given us no descendants but they have left us some of their skeletons, by which documents we can tell what they looked like. Anyone in London can gaze upon the erected figure of the Iguanodon. In 1822 it was dug up in Kent. After a hundred million years it has risen from the grave. Assisted by men's hands and surviving men's bombs, it stands on its hind-legs at South Kensington, a twenty-five foot skeleton (others have been found twice the size), untarnished by time, and ready to march on through the years, its extravagant and appalling aspect a silent and perpetual admonition to bewildered man.

With the neck of a giraffe, the tail of a sea-serpent, the body of a kangaroo, the head of a horse, and the brain of a hen, the Iguanodon hopped on land and swam in the swamps. Possessing multiple rows of grinding teeth it fed upon plants. The amount of herbs eaten in those days is suggested by the equipment of the Trachadon who had two thousand and seventy-two teeth. Indeed the turning of vegetation into flesh was on such a scale that it promoted the growth of the Atlantosaurus who roamed in those regions now lost to the waves. It was nearly eighty feet in length—a territory too extensive to be governed by a single brain. Since the controlling nerves from the head would have had to traverse too many feet of neck before reaching the limbs or establishing communication with the tail, the Atlantosaurus, in common with some other Dinosaurs, evolved a second brain in a cavity within the hinder part of its body.[1] This was the largest of the herbivorous monsters, but the Brontosaurus who made a noise like the advance of thunder was sixty feet long, its footprint covered a square yard of ground, and it weighed as much as thirty-eight tons. The Diplodocus was built nearly on the same scale and looked like an elephant whose nose was its neck and whose tail was a snake. These Dinosaurs, including the Morosaurus of forty feet, and many others were amphibious and may have had some peaceful times in the water when nothing of them could be seen save the neck—a pole giving little hint of the island of flesh below. There they were safe from the carnivorous Dinosaurs on land. But they must have had to face the sea-dragons or fish-lizards. The Ichthyosaurus had a fish-like body without a neck: its limbs were paddles, its nose a sword, its jaws an armoury of teeth, while its eyes, the size of arc-lamps, enabled it to explore the darkness of the depths where it could see for long distances. It dwelt, amongst other places, at Lyme Regis, in company with the Plesiosaurus, or Sea Dragon, one of which found at Ely, had a swimming paddle seven feet long, a jaw of six feet, and a tooth of fifteen inches. These and others, of which there were over fifty varieties, were all air-breathing. So were the Sea Serpents, of which there were more than forty different kinds, varying in length up to seventy-five feet, abounding in North America and at what is now the mouth of the Thames. Though they had teeth in columns of fours along the roofs of their mouths they swallowed their prey whole. They were very like snakes, with arrow-shaped heads. Such was the Elasmosaur whose neck rose twenty feet out of the water while its body was forty feet below the surface.

There may have been birds during this era. At least one is known to us—the Archaeopteryx. It was feathered, and about the size of a rook. There were plenty of flying reptiles. They certainly were not birds, and we may be sure that they sang no songs. They had no feathers, just as the earth-bound Dinosaurs had no fur. They pertained to the condition

[1] See *The World in the Past*, by B. Webster Smith.

of super-bats. These were the Flying Lizards, the Pterodactyls, whose beaks, about the length of a rifle, were set with teeth, and whose out-spread wings in some instances covered as much air as a small aeroplane.

These sea and airborne carriages could keep out of reach of the carnivorous Dinosaurs. Those who remained on dry land had to fight it out amongst themselves. The ferocity of the battles between Dinosaur and Dinosaur is sufficiently signified by the frightfulness of their armour. The Stegosaurus carried upon its back a series of enormous plates resembling a double row of tombstones. Formidable indeed must have been the foes that caused the evolution of such defence. Who could take this fortress? Who enter in at this gate? The Polacanthus Foxi was a walking wall with barbs; the Triceratops was a twenty-five foot boulder; the Scolosaurus, with its cuirass and armoured cape, its ruff of plate, its spiked nose, and its mace-like tail was fit to face the Tyrannosaurus whose teeth were nearly the size of bayonets, and was a match for the Struthiominus who was one hundred and thirteen feet long. Some of the eggs of these plated reptiles have come down to us. The age of mammals had not yet arrived, and these immensities of bone and flesh, these armoured engines of destruction, at first lay confined within the circle of an egg, which was about the size of a super hand-grenade—though informed with a greater potential.

In spite of the fact that the Brontosaurus and others used one brain at headquarters and another at hindquarters, it was yet too little. They could not adapt themselves permanently to the world. But their kingship lasted for what may have been close on ninety million years. We marvel, not at their ultimate extinction, but at the enormous length of their reign. All that time they roamed in the swamps and battled on the plains. They do not belong to history. There is no record of their wrongs. No human eyes saw them, no human mind was confronted by the riddle and the paradox of this clash of life with life for life's sake. From the Jurassic to the end of the Cretacean day they were the highest beings, the boldest expression of Energy organized in earthly envelopes. Then they went down. These vessels perished. The soft garment of silence fell around their fate.

Standing on my hill in Dorset in the pure clear air of the winter's eve, while the clouds, unscantified by history and living to tell no story, passed to their empty destination, I gazed upon the fossils in my hand, the books of stone, and sought to realize the actual existence of that monstrous age to which they joined me. The Dinosaurs did really exist, they did truly trample across the world for ninety million years; but when they passed from the surface of the earth and were seen no more, Man did not yet arise. Not for a long time; not in the Eocene, not in the

Oligocene, not in the Miocene, not in the Pliocene, not for another hundred million years, in the Pleistocene, did earliest Homo appear.

I tried to grasp this reality, this great *fact* of Time. I did not succeed. Once, in the middle of the Atlantic, looking at the horizon, I tried to imagine the space beyond it. For a second I had a true glimpse of that space, and of the space beyond that space. And perhaps for as much as a second now I saw the reality of a hundred million years, and realized how Man, having only had one million years at most, has only just begun his career. But this knowledge soon slipped from me and became merely intellectual. It did not remain organic with me, as is the fact of gravitation or the roundness of the earth. That is our general trouble. The findings of geology are too recent to be as yet incorporated in our consciousness. This weakens the sensibility of our thought. We can be weak in economics; we can be weak in human history; we can be weak in doctrine; we can be weak in literature; we can be weak in many branches of science—and no great harm be done. We must not be weak in anthropology. We must not be weak in geology. The old cosmologies have gone. And because they have gone men have lost faiths and beliefs. They are inclined to despair. There is no need to despair. The message of geology is so inspiring. Our hope and faith should be increased. Consider the main fact. Man has lived a million years: that is all. He may live another hundred million, perhaps a thousand million. We do not spontaneously think in these terms when we speak of posterity; we think of a few hundred years hence—of 2346, not of 22346 or of 2222346. And when we think of the past we feel that the civilizations of Greece and of Rome were a long time ago. Yet in the eye of geology a thousand years hence is as to-morrow, and the age of Socrates as yesterday. These are necessary facts to incorporate into our daily consciousness. Then we should have patience. Then we should have room for hope. We should think sensibly. We should believe in progress—even that! Take our main fact again. A million years ago the ray of consciousness broke in on Man. He stood back, he saw, he became detached. That was a rudimentary ray. There is nothing more obvious than the evolution of our awareness. We are not wiser than Socrates. We are wiser than Neanderthal Man. We are not more ethically inclined than Confucius. We are more ethically inclined than Neanderthal Man. We are not more aesthetically developed than Shakespeare. We are more aesthetically developed than Neanderthal Man. If this is true, it is a tremendous truth: for if the aesthetic sense alone is developing it means that love and peace and beauty and worship and reverence are growing. This has grown—backslidings or not. Another million years will show as much difference again. We may call this faith—it is close to fact. Facts move us, they have much emotional effect, and these facts should inspire us. Our development is attended with sorrow, it is woven with tragedy, it is dedicated to perennial disasters—but it goes on, it does climb upwards. All the arts tell us this. Listen to the symphony! Are we not swept up into the windy mountain passes of the soul? Do we not hear the choir of angels that unspeakably proclaim the unwritten truth?

7. THE UNFOLDING OF THE SEED

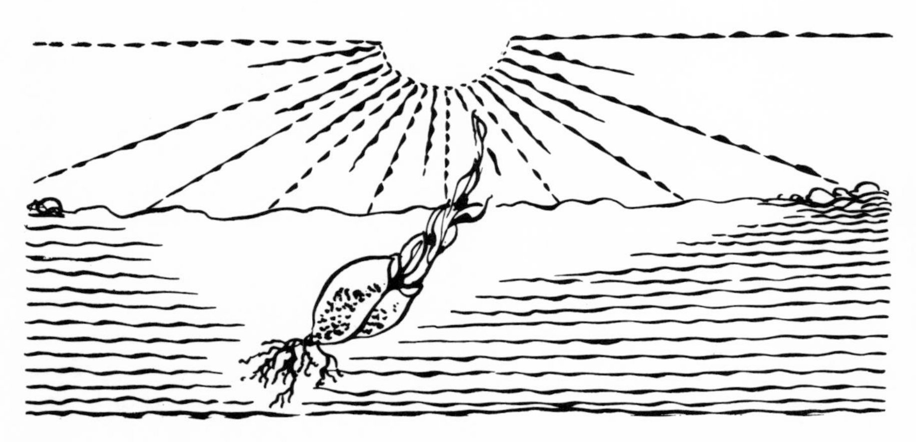

THE corn is rising. The orchards are in bloom. Before the movement goes a step further I am determined to grasp in detail the process of the unfolding. This has gone on year after year around me, and I have admired the performance and paid lip-homage to the mystery of growth. The time has now come for me to follow the workings of the miracle. Anyone in the same state of mind is invited to join me.

The seed—it must serve here as the exemplar of all seeds—arrives in the earth by the agency of man or nature. There it is, ready to start the great work. It is an envelope; or rather two envelopes, in which is confined—a *new birth.* We cannot see this living Principle. It is invisible. It never comes to light, it can never be touched, though it is the hardest of all facts. But we can see the machinery it employs; and having seen it we are satisfied, for we seek no more than the certainty of purpose and design. Within the envelopes are two store-rooms (sometimes only one) containing food to start off with, which we call the cotyledons or perisperm—and this is the nearest we can get to the nascent embryo. At the base is a tiny prominence, the radicle, the beginning of the root. At the top, so incredibly packed that Nature would seem to make zero contain infinity, is a bundle of leaves. And somewhere betwixt and between is another minute prominence, the tigellus, from which the stem sprouts.

Thus seeds are portable dormitories in which repose unborn generations, provided with food when they wake from their sleep. If no moisture gets near them they can remain in their cradles for years, even for centuries, still retaining their power to rise up. Seeds of the kidney bean have been known to sprout after sixty years of rest, while cornflower and raspberry seeds dug from the dry darkness of Celtic sepulchres have grown and flowered like seeds of yesterday.

So we take a seed from its dry place and put it in the earth. If the soil is good various chemical agents therein will immediately begin to act upon the seed, chief of which is water. The moisture softens the envelopes and soaks into the embryo, and straightaway the hoarded provisions are set in motion. One of these rations is a substance called starch. As it stands it is no good, for water will not solve it, and an unliquefied substance cannot travel and penetrate. But there is another substance in the storeroom called diastase which, when water acts upon it, acts upon the starch, turning it into glucose in an excellent state of solution. It is this liquid which now sets the whole outfit in motion, digging and building, so that soon a root is sent down from the radicle and a stem up from the tigellus.

They have most definite and determined natures, these two things, the root and the stem. One seeks the darkness, the other the light. We cannot alter their characters by interference. If we take a seed after the above process of germination has been set going, and twist it upside down so that the root points upwards and the stem downwards, then the root will turn in its course and descend, the stem will turn and ascend. Do this many times, and still the creatures (as we feel them to be) will not alter their determined direction, and will die rather than abandon their cause. Put an acorn in a vertical tube full of earth; let it germinate; let the root seek to explore the darkness and the stem steal up towards the sun—and then reverse the tube. Do it many times, and each time the root and stem will turn right round in their tracks.

The composition of these vegetable parts is not simple like a shaft of steel. There is a complicated but very definite arrangement of fibres, tissues, veins, vessels, channels, and spiral threads all held in place by innumerable bricks called cells which are so small that a host could find comfortable lodging-place on the point of a needle. They are much more than bricks and have many tasks. They are neither solid nor empty; they are bags holding precious properties in a solution which, like blood, is thicker than water.

The root, then, a porous membrane with the above composition, plunges down into the moist earth. It is not alive quite like an animal or part of an animal, not like a claw that grasps or a mouth that sucks—yet very nearly so. Water, which is a thin or weak solution, will always percolate through a porous membrane filled with a thicker solution—this in physics is called Endosmosis. It will also do another thing: it will go upwards, anti-gravitation-wise, by a law of suction if it enters a tube so narrow as to be comparable to a hair; such a tube if placed in a pond will suck the water upwards higher than the level of the pond—this in physics is called Capillary Action. The tube need not be straight, it can be curved, it can be a dense complexity of channels, so dense as to seem like a lump of sugar or the wick of a lamp; yet the water or oil will, on entering a low portion of the sugar or wick, rise to the top. A root provides the conditions for the process of endosmosis and the action of capillarity, and as soon as it is in the moist earth it sucks up water by those two means.

This water which rises upwards against gravitation is called the Ascending Sap.

It is not pure water. For the food of plants must contain in solution some if not all of the following chemicals—carbon, hydrogen, nitrogen, oxygen, phosphorus, and sulphur, plus a modicum of potassium, calcium, iron, magnesium, and sodium. With the exception of carbon, roots can carry up any or all of these preparations from a good soil; and, either through their own intelligence or someone else's, they do gather up precisely those ingredients which they need, rejecting those which are useless or harmful. Yet on examination sap is found to be little more than pure water, the other quantities being incredibly minute in spite of their importance.

Thus we may regard the roots as a colossal network of waterpipes and hoses pumping up tons of water from the soil. I say colossal network, for the aggregate of the ramifications of the roots belonging to one single average stalk of corn is said to be about a quarter of a mile. And I say tons of water, for an acre of corn will on average lift up two hundred and fifty tons a fortnight, while a single elm will in its season raise enough water to fill a tank thirty feet long, three feet deep, and three feet wide.

And yet in spite of all this the plant is not getting enough to eat, and the food which it is getting is not adequately prepared to promote full growth. It cannot go on like this. The stored provisions and the soil's contribution are enough to raise it above the earth; but that done, the part of the building above the ground must help. Brick buildings are built with hands: leaf buildings are built by the leaves themselves.

Since the soil cannot supply all the nutriment, the atmosphere must make up the deficiency. You cannot make things out of thin air, people say. There is no such thing as thin air, if by that is meant something empty. It is really very thick and powerful, and from it all things are made that are made, or without it cannot be made, whether tree, plant, person, or army tank.

What is the atmosphere? It is an air ocean. We walk at the bottom of an air ocean at a depth of from two hundred to five hundred miles. We cannot see it, we cannot touch it, and yet it presses down upon us with a pressure of a ton to every square foot. Each acre of land sustains forty-six thousand tons of air. It is possible to carry this surprising weight on our heads owing to the way it equalizes the pressure all around us. This atmosphere is composed, as everything is composed, of small items called molecules. They are not all of the same kind. Some contain oxygen, others carbon dioxide; some nitrogen, others argon; some ozone, others nitric acid; some water vapour, others ammonia. In quantity nitrogen heads the list and oxygen seconds it, while in importance the carbon dioxide is second to none. When we grasp that water, carbon, nitrogen, nitric acid, and ammonia contribute ninety per cent of all the materials that are built into the tissues of plants, it is easy to see how necessary it is that they should have roots in the air as well as roots in the soil.

The leaves are these upper roots or mouths—plants are pretty well all mouth. Their first appearance in Spring is in the form of knotty bundles, buds—looking like the claws of a dormouse on plum trees, as thin and sharp as toothpicks on beeches, and like half-buried beetles on the twigs of apple trees. In due course they change and open up and throw out what seems a new material altogether, as surprising as if tiny silk handkerchiefs began to grow from one's finger-nails; yet they are wood—thin, pliant, waving wood. The pressure behind this production is the Ascending Sap which, quietly but with great strength, slowly with unperturbed pace like the Hound of Heaven, advances throwing open the green fans. It receives some help from the sunshine, without which in any case nothing could be set in motion; but only when the leaves are fully open can we say that the plant is working from above as well as from below, that leaves are building leaves, and the bars of bough enshaded by their own exertions.

The leaves appear on the twigs in so carefully planned an order that not one overshadows another. Each must get as much sunshine as possible, and their co-operation to this end is such that one leaf never gets in the light of another, but each aims by spiral arrangement at the goal of the greatest sunshine for the greatest number. As one side only is fitted to receive the rays with maximum advantage that side alone is turned towards the sun, and if deliberately twisted over by us, will turn round again with the same unfaltering determination as the root and the stem when treated in a similar manner.

The surface of a leaf consists of a fine shred of stuff like green varnish, which is thus spread with a view to checking too swift an evaporation of moisture. This is the epidermis, consisting of cells each of which harbours two million globular corpuscles called chlorophyll whose green colouring is responsible for the verdant foliage around us, and whose work lays the foundations of the world. The whole epidermis is shot through with tiny holes smaller than the prick of a needle and numbering twenty-five thousand to a square centimetre. These are the stomata, doorways for entrance and exit: of entrance for the atmospheric effects; of exit for the ascending sap after it has deposited its cargo of chemical goods in the ante-chamber of the epidermis to await further instructions.

The blade of the epidermis is supported by a girder called the petiole which rises from the twig. After it enters the blade of the leaf it sends out more ramifications called nervures, they themselves branching out into still more fibres until a beautiful scaffolding is set up. Their task is more than that of a scaffolding; they serve as corridors up which is channelled the ascending sap and down which flows the descending sap after the great operations in the parenchyma. This last consists of a certain tissue of cells in the epidermis which constitutes the supreme laboratory where labour is performed upon which rests the life of the world and the destiny of nations.

Let us consider that labour. The primordial elements of all living things can be reduced to the basic materials of carbon, hydrogen, oxygen, and nitrogen—or even more simply to carbon, air, and water. 'Animals,' says Fabre, 'whether wolves or men, who are not wholly unlike wolves, both as regards food and other things as well, eat their carbon in combination, in the shape of mutton; while the sheep that gives us mutton absorbs its carbon in the form of grass. . . . It is this wonderful transformation which enthrones a vegetable cell as monarch of the world, with men and wolves and sheep as its subjects.'

How does the plant that builds up the flesh of sheep as the sheep goes to build up the flesh of man, consume its portion of carbon? It takes it in the raw. The digestion of its cell is such that it can take carbon neat. Everything living, every one of us must take carbon, for it is combustible, and if we do not burn we die. In order to keep alight our torch of life

we breathe, that is we take in oxygen which burns the carbon which we have synthetically eaten—then we breathe out, we expel the oxygen in combination with the consumed carbon, and the gas is now carbon dioxide or carbon acid. It is a poison gas. We breathe in pure air: we breathe out poison gas at the rate of a hundred gallons a day. All animals do likewise to a certain extent. The air might eventually become hopelessly vitiated and we would perish in our own poison were it not for the vegetable cell which feeds upon this gas, this deadly gas, and purifies the air for us. It is the chief and essential food of the plant, this poison; the cell, that astonishing stomach, exulting in the products of putrefaction, re-creates life from the poisonous relics of death.

The leaf, through its myriad mouths of stomata, breathes in this carbon acid gas, selecting it in preference to oxygen, absorbing it into the tissues of the cells, and conducting it into the laboratory where the labourers immediately set to work to break it up. By some incomprehensible means, under the influence of sunlight, they decompose, the composition separating the oxygen and at once sending it forth into the air again. It entered the orifices of the leaves as an unbreathable gas, it departs purged and changed into a life-giving elixir—a lily, for example, exhaling five hundred pints of oxygen in a summer's day. It will return again with a fresh cargo of carbon to be again purified before once more resuming its aerial wanderings. We, the animals and man, by eating plants and eating ourselves, manufacture carbon dioxide, the poison gas that would choke us even if we used a gas-mask; they, the plants, gladly receive the poison as food and give us in exchange pure oxygen to breathe, while also treating the carbon in such a way that we can eat it.

For what happens to the carbon that is left behind when the oxygen is expelled? Just as the cells of chlorophyll set to work upon it when it came in, so when it is separated they instantly combine it with the ingredients brought up by the ascending sap and awaiting treatment in the ante-chambers. The cavity of that wonderful cell not only decomposes carbon dioxide, it composes new compounds. The carbon is immediately transformed. By combining with the other ingredients gathered from the soil it instantly becomes the raw material of sugar, starch, wood, flowers, and fruit. In this state it is known as the Descending Sap. The ascending sap carried up certain properties. Combined with what has been taken from the atmosphere, those properties, forged in the cellular furnace, have gone to make a final substance which flows down the plant distributing largesse as it goes—leaf-tissue for the leaves; colour and scent for the flowers; starch, sugar, and jelly for the fruit; fibres for the wood; cork for the bark; and gossamer for the roots. Thus the sap's circle is completed.

By mentioning 'flowers' above I have anticipated our story. The buds do not always open into green leaves which set at work those masters in the art of chemistry, the cells of chlorophyll, that weave the wood and build the twigs and feed the whole concern. These work unceasingly for a prosperous present. They care nothing for the future. But the buds also open into other leaves that do not toil and do not spin in that way, and yet are clothed, not in modest green, but in a softer raiment, embellished and perfumed, the admiration of the world. These are flowers. They also work of course—beauty is always incidental—but their work looks to the future.

These flowers are made from the same materials, based on the same architecture, and raised by the same labourers as the other buds. This is the more surprising when we observe how different their instruments are. The following must serve as a general example. Passing our eyes from without inwards we see first a few lovely soft leaves called petals, the total of which is well crowned by the name corolla. Next stand in a circle half a dozen little pillars called stamens, each terminating with a head called the anther, and full of dust called pollen. In the centre is another pillar like a walking stick with a good knob-handle and a sheath at the bottom—this is the pistil, the knob being the stigma, the shaft the style, and the sheath the ovary, which is full of rudimentary seeds called ovules. We should add that the whole flower may be protected by some green tongues called in sum the calyx.

Such is a full flower. Any flower can get on with less than this, with only stamens and pistil if necessary. Thus some plants, lacking the gorgeous paraphernalia of petals, may give the impression that they have no flowers, though all plants have flowers, all plants have fruit, and to talk about flowers as if they appear on some plants and not on others, and to talk of fruit trees as if any tree or shrub could fail to bear fruit, is to suggest that Nature moves with a view to man's aesthetic tastes and gastronomic desires.

The purpose of the erection is to work for the future—to make seeds. Given the above instruments, how is it done? Briefly, by an exchange between the stamens and the pistil: more accurately, by the pollen reaching the ovules and striking up with them the spark of life—which we call the moment of fertilization. Inside the anthers of the stamens the pollen is found in the shape of countless grains each consisting of a single cell with a double envelope harbouring a viscous liquid in which float numbers of minute granulations called the fovilla—for, as we are constantly finding out, Nature delights in the utterly and increasingly minute no less than in the gigantic.

One thing more we should observe since it bears so much upon the pleasure we get from looking at flowers. At various places in the interior of the corolla there are pockets or pouches of nectar in order to attract insects who shall come and disperse the pollen, should the wind fail to do so. And in order to signify the presence of these tempting morsels the petals serve as painted flags.

When the flower is fully blown and the anthers have let loose the dusty pollen to be scattered by the wind or carried by the insects, then the stigma proceeds to exude a liquid slightly thinner than the liquid held within the grains of pollen, so that when the latter falls upon it, it sticks, and while it sticks there the action of endosmosis is again set going so that the liquid of the stigma passing into the grains of pollen pushes out the fovilla, handsomely packed in a painted tube, which, penetrating the stigma and passing down the style, enters the ovary and reaches the chamber of ovules. And then . . . how is the vivifying influence brought about, by what means is the flame of life enkindled? At this point all great scientists are silent and give up the chase, declaring—'No one knows. Before these mysteries of life reason bows, helpless, and abandons itself to an impulse of adoration to the Author of these ineffable miracles.'

Once the ovules have been given life and have achieved the status of seeds, then the life of the flower is over; the beautiful petals that advertised the pollen, the stamens that pillared it, the pistil that received it, fall to the ground, disregarded now in their withered and scarred disgrace of ruin. But the ovary, at first so thin, swells with increasing pride of colour and shape, until it seems to us as we gaze upon the astounding apple, that the petiole cannot possibly bear such a weight without breaking. Finally the seed is loosened and leaves the parent plant, and is dispersed by a hundred different methods across the land.

8. THE PLANT: APOSTROPHE TO AN URBAN GENTLEMAN

It is past five-thirty in the afternoon. For us on the land work is over. We can rest. But when we have gone home, the workshop we have left behind does not close down. We can go home and leave Nature to it, knowing that she will not rest, she will not take off.

Recently I heard a man who was visiting his wife in the country, say —'Give me the plant at home any day.' He was a progressive man with far more use for a piston than a pistil. By the plant he meant the factory, and it was clear that for him factories constituted the only plants worthy of the name.

If Nature were not so silent he might have changed his opinion. There is nothing like noise for suggesting importance. Had we a finer sense of sound we might be able to hear the natural movements. Could he have heard all that was going on around him that man might have been impressed.

Even so, without hearing anything, could such a man contrive to gaze upon the work in progress here with concentrated attention over a period of time, looking down upon it from the Hill of Knowledge, as it were; could he cast his eyes from above the earth to beneath the surface of the soil and attend at the first movement after the seed is sown and see the approach of the water, the cracking of the envelopes, the swelling of the perisperm, the awakening of the embryos from their slumber in the dormitories of the seeds; could he see the translation of the hoarded starch into the magic liquid of glucose from which proceed stems that press up to the light and roots that dig down in the dark; could he see the roots select from the great storehouse of chemical foods flowing within the soil those which they need while rejecting those which they do not, and then under the pressure of endosmosis and by the power of capillarity raise up whole reservoirs of water to the skies; could he see that sap ascend creating as its fluid flows the extra limbs and mouths that soon shall feed the whole; could he see those leaves open out their blades to embrace the sunshine's beaming blows and seek the air for gases while the roots explore the darkness of the earth for liquids; could he see the stomata on the leaves spraying forth to heaven the tented tons of water which have carried up the chemicals into the ante-chambers of the epidermis; could he see those same stomata taking in the carbon acid gas so that the leaves may pasture on our poison; could he draw closer and observe the operations carried out by those master miracle workers, the cells of chlorophyll, in the laboratory of the parenchyma where oxygen is separated from carbon and restored to the atmosphere, where carbon is compounded with other elements and turned into other things, where the hard branches reaching up to the loftiest brightness are first boiled together in this burning cauldron of creation; could he see that sap after its ascension being thus combined and treated then descending through the ribbed corridors of the nervures on the leaves, through the green-paved passages of the petioles, through the fluted pillars and the twisted towers of the stems, down into the roots, distributing good as it goes; could he see these toilers for the present erecting those toilers for the future whose coloured petals and glorious perfumes are the delight of all mankind; could he, still standing on his Hill, still standing there, making use of the divine gift that has been bestowed upon men, the gift to learn, to see, to comprehend something of the Mystery and the Law, could he now turn his gaze upon those flowers in their maturity and see the clouds of pollen borne from the anthers on the wings of the wind or the backs of bees, throw down their fovilla on to the receiving stigmas; could he see the penetration of the pollinic tubes as they pierce the sticky surface of the pistil and then pass down the style into the ovary at the base; could he see this final act, more powerful than that which happens within the perisperm of the grain, more wonderful even than the elaborations in the laboratory of the parenchyma, the final act or the First Act, the moment when the ovule in the ovary becomes a seed, when the spark of a new life is kindled and the Wheel revolves again; could he gaze upon this Plant tirelessly toiling for us and spinning for us, it might happen that he would come to think that it compares not unfavourably with his factory at home.

9. THE IMPERIALISM OF THE PLANTS

ONE July day while hoeing in a bean-field which had become badly overrun with thistles, I was surprised to find myself suddenly caught in a blizzard. The flakes whirled about, very thick, not falling from above but rising from below. It was thistle-seed, of course, which had become suddenly airborne in a gust of wind. A very remarkable sight all the same; and it set me thinking of the various ways by which plants disperse themselves throughout the world.

The great aim of any given plant, it would seem, is not only continuation of the species, but colonization and empire. Few are content with local habitation. They wish to spread themselves across the world. To this end they employ many means of transport. They charter the birds to chariot them across continents and seas. They engage animals and insects to transfer them from place to place. They use floating driftwood and logs and barges on river and lake. They harness the wind and become their own aeroplanes. They surrender to the currents of the ocean and become their own ships. They encourage mankind to administer to their imperial needs. Some even move along the ground unaided.

Let us imagine an island somewhere in the ocean—in the Pacific, say—which has been let down from the sky for our benefit. We will suppose that it had no plants on it. And there we stand, awaiting the arrival of seeds. They will come: for if Nature hates a vacuum, she detests a piece of soil with nothing on it.

Looking out to sea we soon catch sight of a swimmer, making for the beach—evidently a shipwrecked native. His brown head is clearly seen. But when it reaches shore we find that this brown head is really a coconut. The nut contains a large seed packed in oakum and so protected by the strong hard shell that it is safe from the violence of the waves for long periods, voyaging from one island to another, landing and germinating.

Following the coconut many other seeds will make port, their germs protected by every kind of impermeable apparatus, their envelopes turned into boats by pockets of air. Some can sail for over a year and still germinate. Some have been known to cover three thousand miles before their pilgrimage was completed. Others will be shipped to our island on rafts of dead bamboo and sugar-cane, logs and other vegetable remains which glide along in the currents that encircle the seas and wash the shores. It is known that on rafts like these, rats and lizards, snails and slugs and ants have reached remote islands; and it is certain that such Arks likewise lend hospitality to seeds.

So much we might expect, and a good deal more, from the ocean as a means of transport for seeds. At the same time, while they have thus been arriving by sea, others will have confided their dissemination to the winds. For many kinds of plants send their fruits round the world by parachute. We have all seen the dandelion sailing off—its seed ballasting the most delicate aeronautical appliances. Such seeds may go a few yards or a few miles or hundreds of miles. There is no reason why we on our island might not expect a visit from that famous little creeping composite, *Chevreulia stolonifera*, which has been known to carry its message across five thousand five hundred miles from Montevideo to the island of Tristan da Cunha.

Many grasses would also arrive by air. I would hope to see the *Spinifex squarrosus* coming along. Its fruit looks like a porcupine. It can travel by air over four hundred miles, and if necessary cover part of its journey by sea—for the porcupine is so buoyant that it floats very lightly and spreads some of its spikes for sails. Such airborne arrivals would doubtless be followed or accompanied by various spores of mosses and ferns and orchids, travelling from fifty to nine hundred miles to join us.

Thus already our island has been considerably recruited with seeds arriving by water and air. A third service will also be employed, perhaps the most popular—namely, carriage by bird. The procedure is well known. First of all the seeds are introduced into the crop of the bird. To ensure this the plants hold up flags, called berries, to attract attention both as to presence and ripeness of fruit—the red flags being the most popular, though yellow, white, black, blue, and pink are used as the occasion demands. The bird eats the fruit but cannot digest the seed, which in due course will be passed out intact. Meanwhile, safely cabined, it can be charioted across ranges of mountains and arms of the sea. Since over forty different kinds of birds are said to eat any one species of fruit, this bird-mail, however irregular and haphazard in the delivery of its envelopes of seed, can and does make a vast distribution throughout the world. Plants anxious to promote colonization in far distant realms can charter birds that fly up to two thousand four hundred miles. But in this case the seeds do not reside inside but outside their vehicles. They adhere to the feathers by means of hooks and brackets and claws. Or they reside within clods of earth carried away by the bird—a ball of earth which had stuck in the feet of a bird, on being examined by Charles Darwin, was found to contain eighty-two seeds of five different species.

There is one bird which seems to specialize in its planting to such an extent that one might think it deliberate! This is the Eichelhäher in Germany—the name meaning acorn-carrier. It is a famous planter of oak-trees. According to Herr Johannes W. E. Schmoll, it likes nothing better than to carry an acorn in its goitre and subsequently spit it out. It is said that wherever the Eichelhäher plants an acorn it flourishes, though foresters planting in the same area must risk the destruction of the seed by mice or boars: for the Eichelhäher's acorn appears to be distasteful to all acorn-eating animals. The soil of the Grunewald in the Potsdam district was found to be poor for the cultivation of all but pine-trees, and the forestry commission planted only pine; but if you take a walk through the wood you sometimes come across lonely but mighty oaks, which were all planted, according to the foresters, by the Eichelhäher—whose call can often be heard in the district.

After about twenty years our island will have begun to display considerable vegetation in the shape of grasses, shrubs, and even trees. It is not a particularly small island; it is over two hundred square miles, containing mountains, rivers, and plains. There is no feasible spot on this land which the vegetation will not attempt to inhabit; no fertile cranny or crevice into which it will not creep. Thus we must be prepared to see many more devices for transit.

If at any season of the year there are fields of ice or glaciers, then certain seeds like poppy, willow, and saxifrage will *skate* to a further place propelled on the wings of the wind. And plenty of others, with the wind behind them, will be blown across the plains, scattering seeds as they go, and by stages of colonization carry their empire to the confines of the land.

Meanwhile the rivers and the floods will carry on the work of dispersal. At least ninety species will travel by water. Some will drift by themselves. Others, brought on to logs by ants, will be ferried for long distances. But there is one plant which is singular in the execution of its designs—the Lotus Lily. Growing by the side of a river, it creates a wooden basin on the top of its stalk in which the nuts reside. When the nuts are ripe the wooden cradle breaks off from the stalk and sails downstream. And as it travels the nuts germinate and the boat becomes a navigating nursery, a floating flower-pot.

We are assuming that by now this attractive island is by no means devoid of animals. Here is another means of plant distribution. According to the number of animals, we may count additional vehicles for seed. And again it is as if we saw determination, intelligence, will, deliberate contrivance to ensure means of transportation. We are all familiar with the simple burr that clings to our clothes in an embrace impossible to shake off. The burdock growing by the wayside or the goose-grass in the hedges fasten their fruits to anything that brushes against them, be it fur, feather, or cloth. There is a frightful plant called the Grapne which has harpoon-like spikes several inches long, so that any animal lying on one will be driven frantic with pain and will gallop wildly about until it gets rid of it. Certain seeds exude a viscid or glutinous liquid so that they stick to an animal as with gum—to such an extent that a bird gorging on the species *aculeata* can be found lying helpless with its wings stuck together. And of course a sticky seed may adhere to a dead leaf and ride the wind as on a magic carpet.

A considerable number of animals are employed one way or another. The elephant, the alligator, the rhinoceros, the lizard, if handy, will serve; the grasshopper, the termite, and the ant are extremely useful; while the dormouse, the fieldmouse, and the squirrel are inveterate tree-planters, having a convenient habit of storing seeds in the ground and then forgetting all about them. When the sky rains flesh and blood with a plague of locusts there will be another highly favoured means of migration. And, again, birds discharge their duty for short as well as long distances, sometimes whisking seeds from one spot to another at three hundred miles an hour. At the same time, more pedestrian-minded plants, such as the Cacti, may be seen to go by tortoise—perhaps winning the race in the end against another fruit mounted on a hare. The spores of fungi make their excursion by slug, changing later to toad, when they progress faster. Geraniums, stocks, and strawberries may employ the snail, advancing at the rate of one mile in twenty-two days. Some prefer to go by fish. Perch, eels, and cat-fish eat waterside plants and migrate down rivers—often changing from one river or lake to another. Any seed engaging this submarine service must be prepared to complete its expedition by air—that is, if in company with its vessel, it passes down the throat of an eagle, a stork, or a pelican. In the same way an orchid, starting its Odyssey by earth-worm, will frequently continue by blackbird or thrush.

All the plants already mentioned use exterior means for locomotion. But there is one plant which is a pedestrian—the Loranthus. It actually uses its radicle, not as a root, or not wholly so, but as a prop, a leg, a pedestal by which it levers itself to another place. And there are plants which, anticipating the gun and the bomb, *explode* when ripe. The Squirting Cucumber goes off with a bang if you touch it, throwing out its seeds as far as seven yards—while some of these plant-catapults can fire their shot about twenty yards. But let us not forget our well known, well loved, common trees. The twiddling sheath of the Ash rotates sideways to the ground at a reasonable distance from the parent. And no sight in the world is more compelling than a Sycamore seed horsed on the gale, a pair of wings without a bird, a propeller without an aeroplane.

Finally, one last important means by which our island would be fed with seeds—namely by Man himself. When he comes to it he will carry all sorts of seeds attached precariously to the objects of his commercial activity, while he will also bring others deliberately in the pursuit of agriculture.

And so—looking at our island now, with its rich vegetation and smiling fields, what a change is there since we first saw it! Washed by the waves, conducted by the wind, piloted by the birds, seeds have been delivered from all points of the compass. And, having come, they have again charged the wind and the birds to carry on the work of dispersal. They have used the ice and the rivers and the floods. They have enlisted in their service the beasts and the insects and the fishes. They have enrolled mankind to speed their empire and spread their story.[1]

[1] See H. N. Ridley's monumental work, *The Dispersal of Plants Throughout the World.*

10. THE TURNING OF THE WHEEL

THE painter has a start on the writer in dealing with landscape and fieldscape. He can frame his picture, isolate it, and hang it in front of our eyes so that we have to look at it. But the painter can only show us the static picture, he cannot present the seasonal unfolding, the turning of the Wheel. This is where the pen comes in. Painting exists only in space, music only in time: literature commands both time and space.

The harvest is nearly gathered in. I have been passing in review the developing spectacle since March. Beginning with wheat in March, what do we see? The refreshing sight of a brown cultivated field. In April a gleaming green comes on it. There is little to be seen from close quarters; but from a distance, in the morning and the evening sun slanting as it comes and as it goes, that green gleam is like a light, giving rather than receiving rays. This is our second vision, perhaps the best. In May where are we? That illuminated carpet has gone, and a forest of stalks, small pillars of a darker green, have arisen, each culminating in a ribbon—a sort of plume, a pennant, a flag. In June the portion of the pillar immediately below the pennant, looking like a lovely green pencil or fountain pen, begins to swell, It becomes fat. It is not hollow as below that point. It is filled with something which is trying to burst out. And soon a rigging of seeds, no longer enveloped, now develops and rises above the plume, above the pennant which ceases to point upwards and bends over, so that as June turns to July we no longer watch the dark green ribbons on the surface of the corn waving in the wind, for every pennant has been lowered, all those plumes have been cast down, and in their place we see the military, speared, and massed formation of the upright ears. From then onwards until they fall before the knife, the parade is constant, and there is no change save colour: the surface passes from green to grey, from grey to light brown, then to a brown as dark as Hovis crust, even a touch of black at last; the stalks directly beneath the ears being sometimes enlightened by an unacknowledged blue, while farther down the colours become rainbowed in their richness, the charactery in the columns making an evening contrast to the spring-tide shoots at birth, for in a few months they have taken on the weather-beaten beauty of stone besieged and yellowed by the stains of Time.

In the same way the equally disciplined rye stands up presenting the unbending blades in their phalanx on the fields. There is rectitude: there is uprightness. And here is grace; here in the field of oats are seeds as delicately displayed as ear-rings, and when the movement is completed we find imaginary miniature fir trees as alluring as the grassy forests of yorkshire fog. The wheat, the rye, the oats—these, when they have lowered their pennants, thrown down their flags, stand upright till the end. Not so the barley. From the tip of each barley seed a hair grows out and up looking extraordinarily like the antenna of an insect. Wheat and rye sometimes have 'beards' also, but you have to look close. The barley beards are numerous and long. They give the impression of being intensely alive, positive feelers, real antennae, reaching up with the utmost determination to scrape the sky. Thus for May and June. But as the pointed caskets of seed become ripe then the necks of the stalks upon which they are displayed begin to bend, and the antennae cease to pierce upwards. It is at this time that a field of barley shines with that silky sheen that captures and holds our attention beyond all the other exhibitors. The necks give way still more, with swan-like grace bending right round now until at last the antennae point downwards to the earth as if to find the darkness of the grave as surely as before they sought the light of heaven. This is the sign that the hour of the binder is at hand.

I do not understand it. Why does the barley alone need these whiskers? What is their search, and what their prize? If they pick from the air minute potions of life-giving gas, how comes it that the others do without that gas, or do not have to employ such suckers? And why, if the stalks of wheat are strong enough to bear the burden of the ripened ears without bending at all, does the stalk of barley fail to do so, or for what reason does it bow the head? Altogether lost in an ocean of ignorance, I abandon the quest. I am content, though, to stand before these buildings, cap in hand. I could gaze for some time at those wheat stalks alone. Think of the weight of the ears. Nearly half a hundred-weight in an armful. How are the tons in the field thus held aloft by those slender columns of green stalk? Because, we are told, not only is the stem rounded and hollow as with the bones of animals and the pinions of birds, not only is it strongly notched at intervals, but it is impregnated with silicon which is the material that an ordinary pebble is made of. Thus the tons of corn are held as safely on their columns as Nelson on his—for those stalks are made of stone.

Which sight in this unfolding is the best? The first sign of the shoots above ground—at least from the labourer's point of view. As the season advances we become accustomed to the bounty of Nature, we are inured to miracles, and get anxious about the harvest. But the first green uprising on the brown field makes itself felt with the same force as the first warm rays of the sunshine. We have ploughed, manured, cultivated, harrowed, rolled and sown the field. We have done everything possible. We can do no more. Unless we are mistaken we have now set a vast machinery in motion. For several months we need do nothing to the field except roll it; it will do everything for itself until the last moment.

In April those green shoots appear. I do not know whether there are many men, or any at all, who can observe that arrival without surprise. I am not amazed when I see it; but I might well be, and my furthest fathers were. Sometimes when regarding some out-and-out city man who seems capable of taking such a sight for granted, I tell myself that he is not really capable of this, that he also is part of the human race with forefathers who knew nothing of cities. If the sight of the green appearance gives him no stimulus, it must, if dimly, call up some comfort. In the voyages of discovery and invention there can have been no greater moment than when the first man sowed the first seed as an experiment in the earthly laboratory. What can we know of wonder beside that Wonder which was the companion of Fear? We may not know that wonder as we cannot know that fear—nor that hunger, nor that relief. We can imagine; we can recall; we can still stand beside Hiawatha, in a true sense partakers of his wrestling and sharers in his triumph.

11. THE PLOUGH

THE field lies before me. What is a field? I take a piece of it up in my hand. It is not a substance made of one thing like a lump of cheese. It is a mass of small pieces. These are the ruins of rocks: by the play of the atmosphere, by the heat of the sun, by earthquakes and volcanic outbursts, by the motion of the wind, by the rush of rivers, by the action of rain, by the melting of snow, by the scraping of glaciers, by changes of temperature the rocky places of the earth have been laid low and crushed so small that we can hardly see the fragments. Here I tread upon the ancient mountains of the world; beneath my feet lie the solemn peaks that once only to the stars were known, and the cold lunar beams.

In this guise they are remarkably active; for, being informed with chemical properties, they throw off gases and acids and liquids—the first foods. From them grew the first plants. As century pursued century the plants let fall their residuum, spread deep their ashes still holding and multiplying the chemical energies from which the Phoenix of Life rises up renewed and increased in glory and power. This field is a laboratory; it is a storehouse of food; it is a reservoir; it is the nursery of battalions of bacteria in ceaseless chase; it is the habitation of countless worms who swallow it. It is a vast potential.

Yet this field will not realize its potentialities without the help of man—who adds so immeasurably to the beauty of the world. It will lie there, barren and dull. Like many a human being it will remain sterile, ugly, and sad, all its powers stuck and cramped and closed, unless it is released by some liberator. Open it up, let the sun beam down its blows, the water penetrate, the chemicals stir, the molecules move; fertilize it further; impregnate it with seed—and in due season that bare stretch of earth will wave and glitter with so much beauty and intention that the scene will be utterly transformed. So we come to the instrument of liberation, the spade, the moving spade—the Plough.

For the first thing that we must do is to turn over the top of the soil. Then it can be broken up by the harrow. This is the first thing which must be done, which has been done ever since man ceased from simply hunting for food like the animals, and, stepping outside the fatal flow, channelled the force of life to serve his own ends. Thus the Plough holds up the clearest symbol known to man, and is woven into the memory of the race. For this reason the Emperors of China held the plough once a year. The respect paid to it is based on the firmest of all foundations—*need*; at bottom we respect only what we need. Here is a thing we shall always need. It outlasts the marble monuments of princes and even the loftiest rhyme; palaces, temples, towers; factories and foundries; creeds and philosophies; systems of government; great Mars himself in his triumphant car—these hold their day of ascendancy in greater glory, but they fail and fall at last, and are ploughed in.

I was eager to get the plough into my hands—especially the horse-plough. And at length the time came when I stood on the field with a plough and two horses. It lay on its side, for it was extremely like a ship out of water—a ship with a great fish's fin for keel. An awkward hulk to handle until it was launched into its proper element, the earth. The launching and guiding with two horses is of course not easy for the beginner. Yet I got into this extraordinarily quickly and surprised approval was registered on the faces of those who had shaken their heads in scepticism. My striking-out lines were even a success. My main difficulty at first was at the turnings. I began by losing the share, and failing to observe that I had done so—the most reprehensible and amateurish of all mistakes. And it was some time before I could get the horses to turn without stepping over the traces, and prevent the plough from falling on its side. I still felt the need of four hands in order to deal with reins and handles at the same moment.

It was worth any difficulty involved in turning at the ends, if only to see the blade of the turn-furrow come up from the soil flashing in the light, clean as a sword. If we did not 'know' that this happens we might scarcely expect it—that a rusty blade dipped into the darkness of the earth should rise up glittering and burnished! It is always a great moment when the vessel is launched again and becomes light in the hand, while the wave of earth falls away from the prow. In a second everything has come into place; the big wheel and the little wheel in

front are holding a level; the coulter cuts; the share digs; the turn-furrow tosses over the slice. Given level ground and not too many large buried stones, there is no occupation more pleasant and less boring than this. All the body is engaged, and all the mind, while the eye keeps watch on the horses and the plough, fascinated by the way the solid soil leaps up into a seeming fluid wave to fall immediately into stillness again in your wake—a green wave rising when on ley, light-brown on stubble, grey on stony ground. It falls and falls away, this little earthy breaker, until quite soon you see that a section of your field has turned colour completely, and you say to yourself—'I've ploughed that much.' The eye is severely engaged indeed, and yet there is time, and a great inclination, to glance round at the scene as a whole—at the seagulls snow-flakingly following, at the cloud figures, at the sunset as the day closes. I could look down from a certain high field in Dorset into a deep vale which was often filled with sparkling light while we were in shadow. One late afternoon the clouds so gathered that one field below alone received the sun: one lanterned ray enlightened it, filled it completely, not going over the hedges but just down upon that green field only—as if the finger of God were pointing to one page which I must con for truth. I could not con it, being otherwise engaged, but was glad to see the print was there; and glad also, many a time, to glance up as the cold winter day closed down, and see the sunset blooming like a rose, and the tree-top tracery write its hieroglyphics on the lofty scroll.

PART TWO

The Wood

1. THE WOOD AND THE WORK

My task was to clear and thin an Ash wood. It was situated between Iwerne Minster and Tarrant Gunville in Dorset, and belonged to Rolf Gardiner of Springhead, amongst other things a Forester of no mean knowledge and activity. My debt of gratitude to him for commissioning me to do this work and to reap its reward, is outside calculation: I can but dedicate these pages to him.

The last time this wood had been touched was eighteen years previously. It was chiefly composed of ash, though it also contained a considerable amount of hazel, and also some spruce, larch, and oak. In addition there was the eighteen years' worth of undergrowth in the shape of privet and bramble and a great deal of the clinging, climbing, throttling ropes of that hangman's noose called honeysuckle. I could not see into the thickness for more than a short distance, nor advance a single yard unimpeded. As for the ash itself, the trees were of all sizes. There were some very fine single ones, now nearly full grown; but often a clump of five or six rose from one stool, interfering with each other.

My job was to introduce the idea of freedom into this tangle—freedom for the ash. Not for all the ash; only for the best, the straightest, never allowing more than one to remain out of any single clump, and cutting down even good ones if they were too close to others. Darwin said that in Nature the fittest survive. In fact he only showed that those survive who do survive. It is only when Nature is acted upon by Man that the best, the fittest survive. When Man acts upon Man the same principle is not applied. The Spartans alone seem to have pruned our species on principle. We do not do so now, for no one can foretell how great a mind or skilful a hand may belong to a fragile body.

Thus I started clearing and thinning the wood, which covered some fourteen acres. I advanced upon the tangle with an axe, a bill-hook, an ordinary hook, a slasher, a saw, and a pole-saw. Though my chief tools were axe and bill-hook, I used each of the other instruments at intervals, rather like a golfer selecting a suitable club for each new occasion. I put my head down (quite literally) and slashed my way through the undergrowth, brushing up the clinging thorn, the entangling and infuriating privet, and hacking down the honeysuckle's parasitic climbers until I had free play to deal with the trees themselves. Some of them were in very poor shape and it was a relief to get rid of them. But there were many good ones which I had to take down only because they were too close to one another. This sort of thing goes against the grain even when singling mangolds, and in the case of trees it is hard to realize how much room a single tree eventually demands if it is to be a fine specimen. Yet it is a fact that in the first stage of a plantation as many as fifty to a hundred plants may occupy the space taken up in the end by a single mature tree.

The beauty of this job lay from the beginning in the fact that there was so much to show for it. In quite a short time I had made a distinct impression, a definite clearing—the jumble of brambles and shrubs and misshapen trees had vanished from the space I had worked upon, and now just a few straight ash trees stood up clear and free. People speak of 'not being able to see the wood for the trees'. This phrase actually does mean something—(though it might quite easily mean nothing and yet be repeated twice daily by our publicists). It means that a too careful dwelling upon many particulars blinds us from a vision of the whole: you cannot catch sight of the wood as a totality if entangled in the trees. Many botanists are in this unfortunate position. But often the opposite of this is meant. The man who mechanically trots out the phrase that he cannot see the wood for the trees, often means that the confused bulk and muddle of facts confronting him make it impossible to see where his own particular problem stands. He cannot see the trees for the wood. Now that I had already made a beginning, a neat clearing in the wood, I could for the first time see the individual trees.

And as I made a clearing in the wood so also I made a clearing in my mind with regard to timber. As I began to bestow order and tidy up the confusion in front of me, so I began to sort out my odd bits of knowledge about forestry. That is generally my method of advance in matters of this kind. I cannot see, I cannot actualize for myself any department of work unless I have taken part in it myself. I do not possess the politician's and the sociologist's imagination to grasp the actuality without participation. I have to get in touch with it first through work. For me it is first the tool, then the book. I could now take down the word Forestry from its hiding-place in my head and relate it to the world I know.

My first question was naturally very relevant to the work in hand—What is ash used for by man? The answer is that it supplied the material for most of the instruments of husbandry. Perhaps slightly less so now than formerly. An early nineteenth-century farmer declared, 'We could not well have a wagon, a cart, a coach, a wheelbarrow, a plough, a harrow, a spade, an axe or a hammer if we had no ASH. It gives us poles for our hops; hurdle gates wherewith to pen in our sheep; and hoops for our washing tubs.' To-day neither harrows nor ploughs owe much to wood, but we still need it for the other things.

So already an ash ceased to be 'only' an ash-tree in my eyes. And henceforth, when I look across any wood like this I shall see more than trees, I shall see their translation into the familiar objects of the farm and the garden. I shall also see tennis-rackets, golf-sticks, and cricket-bats. Above all—walking-sticks. During some days I had a craze for making walking-sticks myself. The method was so pleasant. Having cut down a tree and observing that it possessed some nice straight branches not too thick for a walking-stick, I cut one off just above the junction of a tributary branch and then cut off the latter a few inches below the terminus. That gave me my handle. Then I measured the stick in my hand against my thigh and made a final cut at the bottom according to my needs—and there was my stick. When I had finished off with a penknife I often had an excellent stick.

2. THE FLOOR OF FLOWERS

APART from any utilitarian considerations, I have always been particularly attracted by the ash whose witch-like fingers with black nails claw the winter sky, and by the aristocratic manner in which the leaves are the last to come and the first to go. The larch, the sycamore, and the horse-chestnut will be in rich leaf without the slightest sign from the ash; the maple, the whitebeam, the hazel, and even the elm, the beech, and the oak are often well away while still the ash remains quite bare is if there were nothing doing this year.

An eighteenth-century forester named Gilpin called the ash 'the Venus of the Woods'. Few would subscribe to this if we think in terms of leaves, since it cannot compare with the glories of the beech or the chestnut; but if we are thinking of a naked winter tree then the ash may well claim to be the Venus of the woods. Its branches are at the top of the tree—a crown—in marked contrast with the oak or the chestnut. Thus you can see a long way into an ash plantation and be fascinated by the beauty of the barks. This lack of low branches and late arrival of leaves provided a further advantage for me—a very important one. I could work in the sun till well into May. Furthermore, the amount of light which ash-trees let into a wood promotes a fine floor of flowers. How vastly different is the other extreme!—a pinewood floor. I used to take a walk occasionally to a little pine wood a short distance away, and look into its daily darkness where nothing grew and no bird sang. In my ash wood the common wild flowers were abundant. They arrived punctually according to the well known schedule. First the primroses in March—when I began work. Then the violets, soon to be overtaken by the anemones who in turn gave way to the bluebells, while the ground-ivy and bugle also appeared, though dog's mercury provided almost the main floor of the entire wood.

We call wild flowers common because of their quantity. But this is just where we strike the great difference between the productions of Nature and the productions of Man. When we produce many samples of the same thing they are of poor quality and we speak of them as mass-produced. The mass-productions of Nature do not fail at all in terms of quality. Take the bluebell. There indeed is quantity. Yet every single year we are freshly struck by their quality. Only a flower-snob could fail to see that any one of those bells on the uplifted belfry is as delicate a construction as any tulip or any rose. I will not say more beautiful, or less, for in this realm of flowers we actually are in the presence of abundant examples of—*perfection.* I think that perfection is the key to the emotion that flowers cause in us. When a thing is perfect the problem of its existence is solved. Gazing at flowers in a wood an unexpected signal seems to go up; we feel a movement of happiness and hope about everything; there is a suggestion that all is really well, all is right with the world, regardless of the geographical situation of the Deity. It is because of this that all men, even ruffians, feel attracted to flowers. For they do intimate to us that, in spite of everything, all is well. Undoubtedly that is what they 'say' to us, and why it cheers us up to look at them. Philosophers say that all the ultimate problems—freedom, immortality, beauty, development—are presented and solved in plants. 'The flora does not only raise, but also answers, all the problems which the human spirit may propound,' said Count Keyserling. 'For anyone who could understand plants perfectly, life would no longer hold any secrets. And the plants surrender themselves so ingenuously to man. No being could be more sincere than they are, more truthful, more genuine. They perhaps of all the world's creatures represent themselves precisely as they are . . . these blessed, pure creatures are never subject to evil moods, and always mirror the very core of their beings.'

Maybe it was because of this that the Sage who sat under the Bo-tree wanted to make plants of men: and we must admit that a Buddha resembles a plant more than anything else. Certainly flowers inspire us: they hold up before us the image of the Ideal. What we would be, could we be true, they are. Ripeness is all. We know that. We see it in the flowers, they are the mirror in which is glassed that goal. But our greatest problem is our unfolding: in nearly every case something goes wrong at one stage or another. We fall. There is no fall of flowers.

3. THE TREE-SHED AND THE TOOLS

EVERY day before I went home I put my tools away in my shed. It had been built for me solely by Nature. I discovered a fairly full grown ash-tree whose trunk was hollow inside at the base for about four feet upwards. There was an opening large enough for me to put my tools through it. Here I placed them every evening, knowing they would remain dry and quite safe since it would be hard to imagine a better camouflage for a tool-house.

In spite of being rotten inside, this tree was in fairly good condition. A tree is not useful to man, of course, as timber, if internally decayed either by disease or the tooth of time; but its own health is not affected if the outer sheaths of the trunk are all right, because the life of a tree resides in and receives reinforcement at its circumference and not its centre. Thus many an Old Village Tree while presenting a magnificent foliage in summer, also provides a huge hollow at the base of its trunk, equally fit as a shelter from storms or a tryst for lovers. Once I saw Mount Etna in full volcanic eruption. It was a sight which held my attention. But at the bottom of the mountain there was another manifestation almost as fascinating—the Chestnut Tree of the Hundred Horses which is said to be the largest tree in the world. Thirty men holding hands do not quite succeed in surrounding it, while a hundred horsemen can find ample room beneath its foliage, as indeed was actually proved when Joan, Queen of Aragon, was caught in a storm nearby and took shelter there with her enormous retinue. And at the bottom of this tree a hole runs straight through, wide enough to admit two carriages abreast. It still yields a good crop of chestnuts.

On my arrival in the wood I took out what tools I needed for the day from this tree-shed of mine. Very often I contented myself simply with the axe and the bill-hook. These are two delightful instruments. There are not many agricultural implements one would speak of in such terms—certainly not of the hoe or the saw. But all good men love an axe; and all Prime Ministers and Literary Prophets in their old age are discovered by the visitor using an axe in the garden. Tolstoy regarded axe-work as a religious discipline. Bernard Shaw declares that it keeps him sane. And it was the axe that inspired Gladstone to say to the messenger who came with the news of his recall to office—'My mission is to solve the Irish Problem.'

I do not know whether there is any absolutely official method of handling the axe. I have no doubt that my own methods leave room for improvement, but I think I must have done the obvious things since in the end my results were good. In cutting down a tree you need to cut low on the stool and to cut clean. A battered, slashed-up stump not only looks unsightly but promotes arboreal disease. Experience taught me to strike down and then strike up, never horizontal, thus carving out a < shape. When I was nearly through I very often went to the other side and with one blow finished the job, or administered a second while the tree was falling over. If the stump then displayed any ragged edges I cleaned it up with my bill-hook. After sufficient practice my wood presented clean stumps and stools instead of a series of wooden clefts and cliffs such as are found whenever a company of schoolboys have been on a job of this kind. I soon learnt not to dash at the thing with undue speed and not to hurl the whole force of my body at the tree, as it were. My technique was somewhat golfer-like. I kept my eye steadfastly on the spot I intended to strike, kept my left arm straight, did not lurch after the axe with my body and only exerted full force at the last minute when also I did some good wrist-work. (Thus I grandly write about my method, and should have done it that way, and possibly, on occasion, even did do so.) I certainly think that the secret of a good cut, especially when dealing with a medium-sized hazel-bush, is in that last golfer-flick of the wrist. I was once held up for a considerable time by a ticket-collector at South Kensington Underground Station who explained to me that his particular and striking ability as a boxer was due to the fact that he didn't put out his strength till the final second of a blow. He was not a big man and he insisted that success in boxing went to the most intelligent, to men like himself who realized that force should be reserved till the last second. 'I box from here,' he kept repeating, and tapped his forehead to indicate the seat of his weightiest weapon in the ring. This unexpected pugilistic tutorial stuck in my mind, and I carried it over with some degree of success into the realm of forestry.

The great thing is to keep the axe sharp. Much depends upon the strength of mind to do this, for it saves much expense of body and spirit. I found out before it was too late (though late enough), that it is an illusion to suppose that one must take an axe to a grindstone with wheel and water complete. The ordinary hand-stone will serve if applied frequently and with a level pressure that does not merely grind the edge but the space before the edge. I used to tell myself to aim at never touching the very edge at all with the stone, but to grind down the rise behind. Given a big stone—not one broken in half—one can sharpen an axe all right and be independent of the elaborate wheel which requires two people to be on the job. For comfort with axe-work, then, I beg to prescribe a sharp edge. And secondly a good axe. That is to say an axe that is neither too heavy nor too light. This is not so simple as it sounds. There are many absurdly balanced axes about: axes with monstrously heavy blades and handles that do not balance them. I bought an axe with a fair-sized blade and a well balanced shaft, and used it with pleasure for some time, till I was offered the use of a heavier axe. At first I thought the latter much better, and when I took up my own it seemed ridiculously light, and on using it I completely missed my aim. But I found that I couldn't possibly keep the heavy one sharp and it became temper-losingly blunt. So I went back to my old axe, and soon it gained in the weight it seemed to have lost, and I never changed again. (Have I any hint regarding a method of sharpening with the stone? Yes, take a stick, lay it on the ground, kneel down and grind away at the blade the edge of which is kept free of the ground by means of the stick.)

Here as in all these matters, to do your job properly and get pleasure from it, you need the good tool. This is equally true of the bill-hook. For a long time I was content with a light, blunt, rattling affair—thinking it all right. But one day I went out and bought a heavier one, a beauty—the gain in speed of work, cleanness of cut, and pleasure in execution being far in excess of the cash value. I generally learn this sort of thing too late, and I learnt this too late since two-thirds of my job was done before I got rid of the old bill-hook. I hadn't realized the difference it would make. The fact is we have in the bill-hook an even more delightful tool than the axe. Especially if you are thinning. You cut down a tree, after which it is necessary to clean it, that is knock off the branches and thus produce a clear pole to be taken away for firewood or any of the other purposes. This is the time when a sharp bill-hook is a joy: a single back-handed slash will generally sever the small branches, while with one or two strokes you can dispatch the larger branches; and if your pole is not too thick and you wish to cut it in half, you can still use your bill-hook for this if it is good and sharp, holding the pole in the left hand and coming down with a back-hand stroke with the right hand. This is an exercise that engages the whole body. It is difficult to think of a more delightful job than this, stripped to the waist in the sun, and thus enabled for a few too briefly passing hours to step aside from the inanities of our repellent civilization. I am writing this account while finishing off this forestry work, and since I am very near the end of the wood the thought of possibly never using a bill-hook again in a big way is very depressing. No doubt I shall be able to use an axe from time to time, and even a plough; but when shall I ever again have a whole wood to thin?

But before passing on I must mention one peculiarity about bill-hooks. They have a way of disappearing. This experience is shared by all woodmen. You are always changing over from axe to bill-hook and vice versa. You put the bill-hook down, take up the axe, and having done what you want it for, reach for the bill-hook again. It has disappeared. Often it is impossible to find it without an irritating search. True, one gets wary at last about this peculiarity and one automatically plans a conspicuous place for putting it down. But, once a more than usually strange disappearance trick was played on me. Near the end of a day's work a shower came on, and leaving my bill-hook I went a certain distance away where there was good shelter. On returning I could not find my bill-hook. In this case there were only ten square yards where it could be, an area not overgrown with anything. I searched minutely and scientifically within that given area. To no avail. It was not there. At last I went home, hoping that on the morrow it would have returned. And sure enough there it was in the morning in the middle of the space I had gone over again and again while searching for it.

4. MEDITATION ON THE STRUGGLE FOR LIFE

DURING my work of clearing there was one thing which gave me particular satisfaction. This was the cutting away of the honeysuckle. Belonging to the parasitic company of plants that engage trees for climbing up instead of rising on their own accord, they often provide grim spectacles in the woods of merciless throttling and strangulation. Ascending from the bottom of the trunk they spiral their way upwards, clinging tightly to the bark. This hinders the sap, the tree's circulation, and after a year or two the young trunk itself becomes a spiral-shaped pole, bulging out in a remarkable manner as if an erect rubber tube full of air had been tightly wound with cord in spiral formation so that it bulged out between the cord (though in the case of the victimized tree or branch the bulge appears *at* the cord of honeysuckle). The tree struggles to live in spite of the stranglehold, but generally in vain. It is apt to die and rot and bend over, a parched ruin upon which the honeysuckle thrives, spurning the base degrees by which it did ascend. I have come upon portions of the wood where honeysuckle had practically taken over: the captive, the twisted, the mutilated, the dying, the dead ash trees stood hopelessly entangled in the network of ropes, pulleys, nooses, loops, ligatures, lassos which outwardly appeared as lifeless themselves as pieces of cord, but were centrally bursting with life and power, ready and willing to pull down the wood.

Mr. Aldous Huxley once suggested that if Wordsworth had lived in the tropics he would not have written about Nature in the way he did. This is pretty obvious. Such speculations are not very fruitful; we cannot move in these hypothetical fields with any profundity. In the tropics Wordsworth would not have written his known work, and perhaps none at all; but that does not mean that men who are native to that clime may not find an approach to a total vision of the Absolute. It also begs the question that if Wordsworth had not been capable of total truth, Nature, in England, as elsewhere, provides ample opportunity for the half-truth. The king of the half-vision is that other lordly and everlasting bard, Thomas Hardy. In one of his forest descriptions in *The Woodlanders*, after speaking of Nature's merciless battles, he adds—'Here, as everywhere, the Unfulfilled Intention, which makes life what it is, was as obvious as it could be among the depraved crowds of a city slum. The leaf was deformed, the curve was crippled, the taper was interrupted; the lichen ate the vigour of the stalk, and the ivy slowly strangled to death the promising sapling.' I came across the same sort of thing every day in my wood. It could make me silent and it could make me sad, but personally I cannot see the spectacle in terms of unfulfilled intention save superficially. What I see is—an almost liquid surging up of life. I see that life as a massive unity, moving and flowering under the influence of Fire—the air itself taking visible shape in the plants. Some of it does not get up, all of it cannot get up. But if one tree succeeds, one baby survives, I applaud.

Thus, even when we are feeling gloomy, philosophy will keep breaking in, with its happy, glancing gleam.

The spectacle in my wood which fascinated me most, and encouraged me most, was—decomposition. As I hacked my way through the undergrowth I came upon many fallen trees which had been lying upon the ground for years. They lay there presenting every variety of rotting trunk and bough, in every stage of transition as they slowly burnt their way back into the ashes from which the Phoenix of Life rises up again. I would take my bill-hook and cut into a trunk lying covered with moss. It would go in deep, as easily as into a lump of cake, until it struck abruptly the inner part not yet decayed. I would take out slices, letting them crumble in my hand and fall to the ground—as *humus*. Once a seed, then a sapling, then a great hard tree, now softly turning into *earth*. I found them, I say, in every shape and style, lying in the silent shades in a melancholy mightier than beauty. At a touch a branch would fall, already dust. Under my feet a weeping clod of wood damply squelched like wet paper. Deep, soft, dark green moss covered nearly every limb, like velvet on old discarded furniture. Age or storm had laid these low, but there were also stumps where full-grown trees had once been sawn off. I was never tired of testing their present status with my boots. Some were still hard as a table, with perhaps a large fungus growing on them, nearly the size, colour, and shape of an elephant's ear. Others, enmossed inches deep, were as springy to stand or sit on as an armchair. Some had almost wholly conformed to the law of return and scarcely differed in appearance or material from the earth around. Others made magnificent portals and main entrances to rabbits' burrows.

Sometimes I knelt down beside one of the most ancient trunks, and peered under the bark and into the caves and recesses and cups that marked the erosion of time; and there I found colonies of insects building their Jerusalem in these countries of decay which must represent for them the acme of perfection. And there also fungi, like jellyfish, like sponges, like rubber flowers, took life-giving elixir from the burning bark. And as I sat and leaned and looked upon these lands it seemed to me that here too was blessedness and peace, and glory though it did not shine, and innocence untainted as the new-born babe. Here might the weary and the sick come and lay them down; and without anguish, and without misgiving, fall back and return to the ashes that never die.

5. THE VIRTUES OF HAZEL

As I advanced, the terms 'hard-wood' and 'soft-wood' began to mean something definite to me now, for the difference in resistance to the axe was decisive. There were a few spruce-trees at the edge and my axe sank into that wood very easily. The extreme softness of young oak surprised me. The hazel was by no means as hard as the ash. All the same I was puzzled by these terms; for we all know how hard the oak is when seasoned, and the spruce becomes excellent, I understand, for rafters and boarding, ladders, props, and packing-cases. That miserable tree, the elder, which occasionally I came across, can be cut without effort, but seems to become harder even than any of the others. The axe makes a different sound against each species of tree, and a skilled woodman ought to be able to tell from a distance whether, say, an ash or a hazel is being cut down.

It is easier to get your axe into a hazel than an ash; but it is much harder to get at the hazel. It gave me little pleasure to come upon a row of hazel-bushes to be cut down and laid. The hazel does not aspire. A dozen shoots from an ash-stool will all seek the perpendicular, and the most favourably placed amongst them will stand up straight and high. But the shoots, fifty or more sometimes, from the hazel-stool, while they *start* straight, later begin to fan out, and even the one at the centre makes no attempt to grow straight, and all the branches intertwine tremendously. In short the hazel is a bush, not a tree; and a bush is a tree whose shoots thrive in concert and together make the unit. The hazels' quick growth, abundance, flexibility, and thinness make them one of the most valuable of all timber crops, since they can be twisted so easily into fences and hurdles, while their tributary twigs are the very thing for bean-stakes.

I imagine that they are also excellent for fishing-rods. I do not know whether this is officially right but I think it must be, because certain branches that I handled *were* fishing-rods. While at work I caught fish with them in my own peculiar way. When you cut down hazel you do not clean it for firewood or poles (unless the bush is hugely overgrown with shoots the size of small trees). You lay the branches on the ground all facing one way, placing each branch behind and half over the previous one, so that when you are dealing with many bushes you make a long line of sloping hazel branches like a kind of hedge which is called a drift. It is pleasant to transform the tangle into drifts running parallel through the cleaned-up wood. But to lay them thus is not very easy. The numerous tributary twigs of hazel-bushes are so intertwined that when you start to extract the branch you have just cut off, it is no easy matter getting it free from the main clump; and if you have left anything within reach on the ground, say a coat or a hat or a handkerchief, then often the terminal twigs of the extracted branch, bending down, will tend to scoop up your property. Once when struggling to lay a long flexible rod beside the other branches on the ground, I hooked up my hat exactly as if it were a special kind of fish. I mention this trivia because it is my only fishing story, and it would seem to suggest that here is the perfect material for the complete fisherman's rod.

It serves another purpose which also may not be official. It is splendid for the amateur chimney-sweep. Nowadays if one wants anything done one must do it oneself. To be my own plumber is quite beyond me, and when my only tap—a short one from the rain-tub to the copper—split in a frost, I never had even that one tap to use. But having once set my chimney on fire I saw that in future I must keep it swept. So, taking a tip from a countryman who is full of ways and wiles, I did my own sweeping. The tip was to select a long hazel-rod of fair strength and much flexibility and take it home. Then tie a number of sprigs of holly round the thin end. This was the sweeping-brush. It was too long to fit into the room, so one just let it in from the door or window and then curved it up the chimney. Such a rod easily reached to the top of my chimney. As I cleaned lower and lower I cut the rod, thus greatly facilitating the thoroughness of the brushing. By this means the soot came down perfectly. Half-an-hour's job. And having taken the precaution of wearing gloves, an old hat, and mackintosh, I did not emerge from it in the least grimed. I do not say that this would work in a big house, but it is the chimney-sweeping solution for anyone with a cottage in the country; and so I think we must definitely give such brushes a prominent place on the list of the hazel-tree's gifts to mankind.

6. IN THE PRIMEVAL CHASE

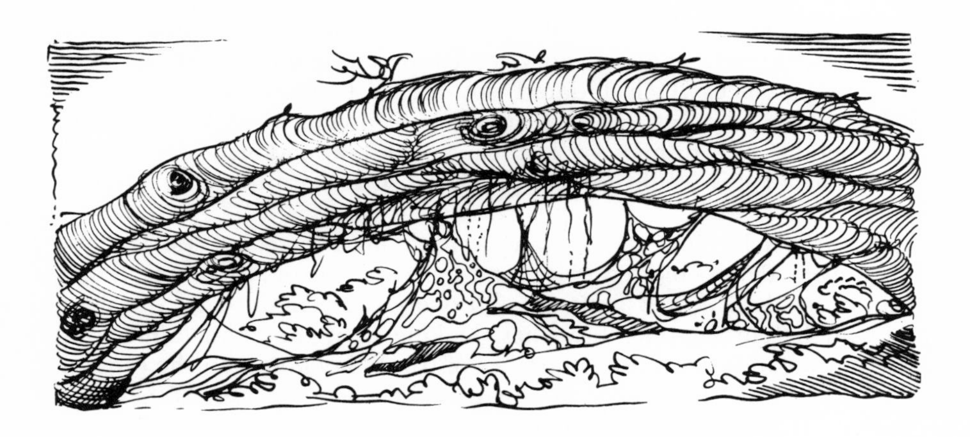

THE atmosphere of the wood was entirely altered by my intervention. It became a different place: not the same place altered, but as different as if on going down a lane to see a certain wood in a given county, you came upon another landscape. There was now no disorder; the trees were visible, and (before I had done) you could look for a long way in all directions through a small forest, whereas before you could only see a few yards. Space and light and orderliness had been introduced. It now seemed more alive, happy, and beautiful—from the view-point of man (who sticks on the labels). And since we do stick on labels it is a sad ineptitude to suppose that Nature cannot be improved upon from a 'beauty' point of view, by man. The idea that 'every prospect pleases, while only man is vile' is not the whole truth. Man has added to the beauty of Nature in as measurable a degree as, say, between an area of uneven, tufted, coarse grass and a well-tended lawn margined by geraniums.

I often used to think of this when I strayed beyond my wood into further forest-land, especially one portion which seemed to have been neglected for centuries. It was a gloomy place at most times of the year. The trees were chiefly oak with some silver birch. It was like walking at the bottom of the ocean and continually finding some wrecked vessel. Or again, like coming upon the scene of a battle waged long ago: huge corpses of tree-trunks sprawled on the ground, their limbs like the broken arms of giant men lying where they fell. From some ancient oaks, a great branch, through weight of years, violence of storm, or stroke of lightning, had cracked at the fork and the branch leaned to the ground—a giant arm with fingers gripping the earth. Often it seemed as if I had visited the place of some terrible calamity long since closed in the withered page of history, and now made ghostly by the ever-reigning silence which I dared not break. I could see little of the greenery above, but walked submerged down there amongst the dereliction and dismay of lost causes and abandoned hope. How different all this would look, I pondered, if it were taken in hand by man.

The silver birch were not doing well amongst the oak trees. Many of them were dead—blasted poles erect in the foliage of other trees. Some, still in feeble leaf, had begun to fall over, and remained on the slant, upheld by surrounding branches, looking as if they had fainted but were just caught in time. A number of trunks lay about on the ground, short pieces nearly covered over by the dog's mercury. One of these had a hole in it which ramified in several directions, at the entrance of which was a damp, round fungus; or so I thought, till I noticed it was breathing, and saw it was a large slug. This old trunk lay at the foot of an erect log—I cannot call it a tree for the trunk had broken off about ten feet from the ground. There it stood now, immensely lichened and mossed, a shaky column with one exceptional feature—it had steps placed in spiral-shaped form going up. They were small steps but very attractive in their wonderful colour congruity with the weather-washed, old, white-patched bark of the birch. Had they been firm enough they would have served me admirably for climbing up to examine the top of the column. But they could hardly hold me since they were made of fungus. Nevertheless I have never seen more definite and attractive steps than those upon that tottering tower.

It is not surprising that there was an ancient atmosphere about this place, for I was working in the middle of Cranbourne Chase. At one time it had a perimeter of over eighty miles, from Shaftesbury to Salisbury on the North, and encircled by the Stour and the Avon at the other sides. Now it is shrunk to a small oasis of wild country. But that oasis has changed little in the course of centuries. It remains, as Thomas

Hardy has written, 'a truly venerable track of forest land, one of the few remaining woodlands in England of undoubted primeval date, wherein Druidical mistletoe is still found on aged oaks, and where enormous yew trees, not planted by the hand of man, grow as they had grown when they were pollarded for bows'. Wandering here I could well feel that if the world is too much with my fellows it was not too much with me. In the strange days in which we live I could actually say farewell to the world far more effectually among these shades and natural debris than on any island in the Pacific Ocean.

I decided that if ever I were a fugitive from the Law this is where I would hide. But I learn that this decision of mine is not strikingly original. In fact, before 1830, the Chase had become so popular as a smuggler resort, and so sought after by thieves, murderers, and criminals of every grade no less than by poachers, blackmailers, tramps, and vagabonds, that in the end it was treated as a covert for crime, and was disafforested.

7. BRACKEN

You have to keep your eyes open in the country if you want to see the spring before it is all over. This is borne in on me every year. The whole affair is so swift and so variegated that unless we are careful we miss half of it. During some months of summer and some of winter the casual eye sees little change, but during April and May the speed of appearance and disappearance is almost on a par with the cinema. One wants to see the show through again at once, and get the order of things right. Nothing requires more deliberate intellectual exertion than to follow the unfolding closely, nothing more time-eating. I found it much easier just to get on with my job of thinning, and I often put off looking at something until 'later'—by which time it was gone. Luckily the flowers do not all appear quite at once. The primrose path has time to make an impression before it becomes the property of bugle and ground-ivy; the celandines, the anemones, and the violets have fallen before the bluebells rise to spread their gospel and then yield to the aristocracy of the foxglove.

In this wood it always seemed to me at one period, near the end of May, that everything would have to give way to the empire of dog's mercury. But of course this was reckoning without the bracken which steps in and takes control from June onwards. Here indeed is a case in which you must keep awake if you are not to be surprised at almost an apparition. For the unfurling of these fern-flags from their unnoticed beginnings to great thickness and height is one of the swiftest of all the transactions. The leaves are packed in a roll very much like those things you find in Christmas crackers and blow out. And they unroll so swiftly that their internal chemical apparatus might seem to have the force of steam. Unlike ordinary ferns and all the other plants around, they continue to grow higher and higher until six or eight feet is not uncommon. A miniature forest has suddenly appeared in which a child might get lost.

Farmers can very seldom enjoy aesthetically what they deplore agriculturally, and since bracken has a very bad reputation as a particularly injurious weed, we seldom hear anything good of it. But a philosophic mind, uninstructed in the claims of agriculture, might well conceive the frond in a favourable light. For it is a direct descendant of those Tree-Ferns that once covered the whole land of Europe before bird, quadruped, or man appeared. The atmosphere was then unbreathable, containing in suspension in the state of poisonous gas, the huge mass of carbon which has since become coal. The tree-ferns cleansed it. They subtracted the carbon, storing it in their leaves and stems. They continued this atmospheric purification for generations, and when at last they died their buried remnants became coal in which even to-day we can find many leaves and stems wonderfully preserved, archives in which we may read 'the history of this ancient vegetation which has given us an atmosphere that we can breathe and has stored up for us in the bowels of the earth those strata of coal which are the wealth of nations'. Fabre, from whom I quote those words, traces bracken as descending from that noble line, and states that 'the stem of our common Bracken reproduces in its bundles of blackish, lignous tissue, the rather sketchy design of a two-headed, heraldic eagle as though to blazen the nobility of its ancient race'.

And should the man of philosophic mind, while contemplating these things, fall into a less elevated mood and inquire whether it was really worth while for the ferns to cleanse the air of carbon poison gas if we, the inheritors of their bounty, prepare a poison gas of our own to destroy ourselves, he may still reflect that Necessity, so aptly called the mother of invention and discovery, has in these latter days found uses for bracken unsuspected by our ancestors. Thus the Glasgow Research Station finds that silage can be made from it. Mr. Ronald Duncan cooks it as a kind of asparagus. Dr. Krebs of Sheffield University claims that yeast can be made out of it. The Germans make petrol from it. Silage for stock, petrol for machines, yeast and salad for men—not bad for a weed.

Not bad; and a hopeful sign of the times with regard to the future. A new principle is beginning to be advanced—that of each country making use of its own resources before dashing off to the ends of the earth for new materials. Hitherto we have tapped our own resources only to a small extent, and when we saw something in a far country we built a ship and went and got it from there. Other nations have followed suit, all trying at once to procure the rare substance from the far place, and claiming 'equal right' to do so. That was called Imperialism. To-day a new possibility opens. Science steps forward demonstrating in a remarkably concrete way that since all things are all things, almost anything can be made from anything. Before our astonished gaze they turn wood into jumpers, milk into buttons, maize into mud-guards, glass into shirts, bracken into petrol. The dream of the old alchemists is surpassed and transmutation becomes the order of the day. No longer shall Imperialism be necessary. No longer shall men, in the name of trade, in the name of religion, in the name of civilization go to Persia, to India, to Honolulu in order to steal away some local treasure. They shall stoop down and find it at their feet.

In the meanwhile I am more content to regard bracken as bracken, and not as petrol or anything else. Indeed I fear that if I am right about future developments, men will look at phenomena even less than they do to-day. To *look at* the object, at any object, and see it in its own right is the key to a fuller apprehension of the mystery and significance of life. But there is no money in this, and so people do not bother to use their eyes in that way. Perhaps in the future they may look at the object more closely—but only with the motive of turning it into something else.

Let me look at my bracken here, I said to myself, without ulterior motive or agricultural disgust, and watch it spring up mushroom-like before my very eyes. Most of the flowers have already faded and now they are disappearing beneath the ferns, and the great kingdom of dog's mercury no longer usurps the scene. And as I gaze at it I gaze back across the years of my iife and see again the tall bracken in the lonely glen on the Wicklow Mountains through which deer and stags leap with amazing speed.

8. OLD AND NEW ATTITUDE TO TREES

THIS wood had been neglected so long that I came upon great waste of potential timber. Here and there a full-grown tree had evidently crashed down upon surrounding shoots. I occasionally found a trunk or a big branch lying right across a stool from which ten shoots were growing. All would be twisted, none worth keeping there. Many of these young ash-trees had thereby assumed the strangest shapes, for they had had to twist themselves as if they were made of rubber. Sometimes they looked like the neck plus the head of a swan, and I saw one that reminded me of that queer flamingo that Alice used as a croquet-mallet in Wonderland. Some had twisted their way up snake-wise in order to pass the obstructions. Some were linked in close embrace and one had grown in such an extraordinary way that it now *ran through* a larger stem. I could do nothing in such places but get rid of all the twisters and leave an open space.

At other times I came upon three or four excellent trees, all straight, all doing well, all big and high. But since they were too near to one another, only one could be left standing, and I had to select the best. I was often in a real quandary in deciding which was the best, for just as at one place I would find three to five twisters close together, at another I would find an equal number of champions.

When it was thus necessary to axe a beautiful ash-tree for no better reason than that it was too close to another one, I felt extremely apologetic. For trees do exert a strong personality. It is said that in certain parts of Austria there are still to be found peasants who beg the pardon of a tree before felling it. Sir James Frazer told how the in-

habitants of Sumatra used to lay the blame at the door of the Dutch authorities. A native would go to a tree which he had to cut down in order to make a road, and would pretend to pick up a letter which he then read aloud to the effect that the Dutch authorities enjoined him to fell the trees. . . . 'You hear that, Spirits,' he would cry, 'I must begin clearing at once, or I shall be hanged.' The seriousness of tree-worship in ancient Germany brought ferocious penalties upon anyone who peeled the bark off a standing tree: his navel was cut and nailed to the tree, and he was driven round and round it until his guts were twisted about the trunk. Plutarch relates how the withering of a sacred fig-tree in Athens or Rome was regarded with consternation; while if a tree was observed by someone to be drooping, a hue and cry was set up and people rushed to its assistance with buckets of water as if to put out a fire. At many times and places it was considered essential to make sacrifices to trees sometimes with fowls, and sometimes with human beings. If we bear in mind the many beneficent qualities ascribed to trees in the past, it is easy to understand why a custom like the May-tree or the May-pole prevailed. In Spring a tree was brought into the village amidst applause and rejoicing, the intention being to bring home to the village and to each house the blessings which the tree-spirit had the power to bestow.

Mankind dominates the world to-day. It is certain that trees once did so. It is not possible for us even to imagine the immense forests that existed at the dawn of history—when clearings were but tiny islands in the atlantic stretches of wood. In the First Century the Hercynian Forest stretched eastward from the Rhine farther than any man knew: men, questioned by Caesar, had travelled for two months without reaching the end. I like to think how the Weald of Kent, Surrey, and Sussex are remnants of the great forest of Anderida that once clothed the whole of the south-eastern portion of the island, joining another (older than the Chase or father of it) from Hampshire to Devon—and how in the reign of Henry II the citizens of London hunted the wild boar and bull in the woods of Hampstead.

However, since the days of tree-domination and tree-worship we have progressed so much that we now can see them in terms of £ s. d. When I cut down a tree I had levelled a piece of 'timber' valued at so much a foot. During many a five minutes I have knocked out about a shilling's worth a minute. I stacked the poles neatly in piles of a hundred—(my own pay being so much a 'lug'). One day a timber-merchant came to the wood to decide what he wanted to buy. He was accompanied by the foreman of the estate. Together they arrived at the just price. Then the timber-merchant inspected a portion of the wood not yet tackled by me, marking specially straight trees that he fancied. I said in an aside to the foreman that not all the ones the man was marking could rightly come down, and the foreman said to the merchant at intervals—'But we must look after our own interests.' The man took no notice and continued marking trees while we looked on disapprovingly, the foreman repeating—'Of course we must look after our own interests.'

When the timber-merchant had gone, the foreman, an unexuberant personality, looked round at the wood, appraising it. 'There baint nothing in trees,' he said. I made some kind of commercial remark. He looked round at the wood again and finally dismissed the whole prospect with two weighty words—'It's *dead money*,' he said. Having brought forth this gem of ages-old wisdom he gazed over the wood sourly and mournfully as if filled with sorrow at the sight of so much dead money.

9. CLOTHES AND SANITY

It was not until the bracken had started to appear that the roof was put on the wood. Since the ash does not send out its branches till near the top, we do get this effect of a roof in any reasonable ash wood. Visualize a larch, a chestnut-tree, and many a beech and oak, and then remember the tall, bare trunks of the ash branching only at their crowns, and you will grant that it is indeed the placing on of a high roofing that we witness in May and June. It was pleasant to look through an acreage of bare trunks that I had disentangled from the press of competition, and then up at the intermingling greenery enlightened by the sun. You can seldom get this effect from other trees growing together. The chestnut branches out very low, and while beeches do often present a high, lone stem they often do not, and you see beautiful leafy branches sweeping the ground; while the oak, though also capable of the long clean trunk, goes in for great thick limbs sprawling out parallel with the ground or twisting upwards from a low fork. However, I must not run my image of columns upholding a roof too far in connection with my ash, for there were many gaps of course between the crowns, and also a number of blanks owing to lack of trees.

I welcomed these gaps and blanks, for otherwise I had to work in the shade far too often. And when the sun is shining I do not take kindly to working in the shade. Give me heat every time, I do not mind how much. I can do twice the amount of work in the sun than when away from it, or clothed off from it. This is partly due to my attitude towards clothes. I like to wear the right thing in the right place, and am no advocate of unconventional attire. But the right thing, at certain times, in certain places, for many people, is often a pair of shorts and nothing more except for the feet. For many agricultural jobs that is not the right thing at all, but for some it is. As for axe-work in the summer, and bill-hook work while cleaning your fallen tree, it certainly is right when the weather is hot or muggy or showery. Thus unencumbered I can do, and like doing, a week's work in two days. The hotter I get the harder I work, perspiration making me almost cold and the sun not hot enough to make me even feel its heat then. The sheer freedom of the limbs with the breeze on the body gives a pleasure not easily excelled; one could justifiably enthuse about it; I content myself with saying that though this is not the only way of feeling happy and alive, it is one way. To use the mind at full concentration is one of the most manly things we can do, since this capacity happens to be the special gift of man; but we are also animals, and we experience great joy when, in primitive surroundings, we are not dolled up and tied down with artificial skins. Thus with me anyway; I cannot exaggerate the satisfaction I get from becoming a 'savage'—even in colour. And I fear that many a Lancashire young man—need I say 'lad'?—having come home from the Far East, will miss, at intervals throughout his life, sometimes quite savagely, his shirtless army days in the jungle.

There exists a strange crowd of people called Nudists. It might be thought that here we have sane people in an over-civilized world. But this is not so. They are misled. They imagine that by simply taking off their clothes they can side-step the sophistications of metropolitanism. Yet of course they can do nothing of the sort, they merely become unclothed and in their wrong minds. Once I turned off a main street in London, and having paid a fee of two shillings, was admitted into a large house in which a nudist gathering was in progress. When standing in the porch and glancing round at the pavemented vistas of the metropolis, I felt surprise at the assumption that inside this house it would be possible to 'return to nature' by the mere removal of clothes. And having entered I did not find the scene or the proceedings in any degree inspiring. There was one room reserved for games, though no particular games were being played and people were wandering about in it aimlessly since there was no possibility of exercise of an exacting sort. Most of the members were in the next room—having tea and cakes. No one wore anything. This looked incongruous in the electric-lit room with its tea and cakes and the people sitting in rows—idiotic might be a better word. And should anyone have come along, I reflected, with an erotic *arrière pensée*, he or she would quickly have found that nudism is the enemy of eroticism (though possibly not if everyone wore a mask). As I had entered fairly unnoticed it was easy to slip away without offence, and I was glad indeed to regain the comparative sanity of the city streets.

The point is that these nudists run a principle—no clothes: (and this insistence upon none at all is an indignity). It is just a thoughtless principle with no sense in it, seen in practice to be far the most unnatural and unsane affair in the whole city—a sort of climax of absurdity. The more reasonable, open-air nudists do at least enjoy the sun. Unfortunately they sun-bathe. That is to say they *lie about* doing nothing. In moderation that is all right, of course, but done in company and as a great thing in itself, it is pretty miserable. The whole thing is done too seriously and too thoroughly. One should avoid thoroughness in such fields. My own principle concerning the whole matter is simply this—that the way to enjoy the sun is through working in it or playing a game in it, and that there should never be the raising of an eyelid if a shirt is removed in any congruous setting. But to-day we still have crazy people who think nothing of a bather approaching the sea in bathing-shorts, but would stare at a cyclist going up a steep hill on a hot day in shorts only. And then over against this we have the lunacy of a whole-hogging nakedness carried even into a city mansion during a winter evening!

In my wood it was unnecessary to consider the existence of either sort of person. I could do the natural thing without the slightest botheration. Much of the work was really strenuous. There were trees to cut down large enough to merit two men with a saw; and when I had axed them down, and cleaned them up, and then chopped them into poles short enough to load on a lorry, I arranged them in piles of a hundred. All this was wonderful exercise, the axing and the hauling about requiring full strength, while the branch-cleaning with the bill-hook as I held up the heavier branch with one hand, engaged every muscle in the body. It gave me unbounded pleasure to go at this furiously for hours on end if the sun was blazing down on me. It didn't matter how hot it was, the hotter the better, for then I became very wet with perspiration and needed the warmth of the sun as one coming out of water, while if it rained the drops melted at once. Thus dressed I often felt that I could go on all day without exhaustion, whereas in the winter I couldn't do a third of the work in the time. I used to smile sometimes at the thought that I was being paid to enjoy myself thus, in a world where a boss who says—'I'm not paying you to enjoy yourself, my boy!' is considered a particularly reasonable and high-minded pillar of society.

10. THE GARDEN OF EDEN

THAT was one peak of pleasure. But I got as much out of sitting down for my breaks. To be tired enough to make the act of sitting down a sensation of real relief, is a pleasure which has much to be said for it. And provided that you are not over-exhausted but just physically in need of a rest—then the mind often functions at its very best. After some food, hot tea from the thermos, and a cigarette, it is quite remarkable how freely the brain can move, and how favourable the conditions are for unpremeditated meditation.

There is one more proviso for me—the perfect seat in a sunny spot: or in a shady spot at those hours on certain summer days when the sun is actually too hot to sit in. I was expert at finding such places. I kept finding new ones, thinking each better than the last. By a perfect place I mean a tree which I could lean against comfortably and which was so situated that other trees would not block the sun at those times when I would be sitting down. As I say, I found several, and shall remember them all my life because of the happiness I found there and the glory that shone round me. There was one outstanding tree at the foot of which I took up my position very often. I did not cut my way towards it for some time, but when I had discovered it I made it my headquarters for meditation. Trees are particularly conducive to meditation: no doubt that famous Bo-tree did much to prepare Gautama for his hour of enlightenment.

This particular tree was not an ash, it was a fine old oak. Its trunk had considerable girth—three men holding hands could hardly surround it. At about three feet up it leant out and forked into such large branches that it was a question which might claim to be the trunk. At this fork, and for some distance along one of the branches, a fern garden was flourishing. (This arboreal garden was very delightful to contemplate in the summer. A maple-tree, not far off, had a mistletoe growing on one of its branches, and on my way to Blandford I used to stop and look at another maple where to my amazement I saw a young silver birch growing healthily in a moist niche high up.) The arrangement of branches was such that no great limb immediately roofed me blocking out the sun, but at a suitable height the leafage was so plentiful that as a shelter from rain this was perhaps the best tree I have ever known. That leafage, combined with the trunk which gently sloped outwards over me, prevented a drop of water from falling on me for quite a long time even when it was raining heavily outside. I say outside because on such occasions I could sit as if I were indoors without the slightest necessity to put on a coat. It was curious to see the rain pouring down while I, though out-of-doors, was really in-doors. It would be half an hour before the roof would begin to leak a bit.

The situation was not altogether perfect with regard to the sunshine, for after ten o'clock in the morning a big tree intervened. But up till then it was the best place in the wood, and during really hot weather it was superb for thoughtful shade. If there was wind at other places there was no wind here, for I placed 'drifts' either of hazel or of branches cut from my ash-poles, at each side. And finally, it was easy to lean against: the earth was soft and no roots stuck out; instead there was a sort of alcove into which I could fit and lean back so as to be comfortably upright.

I mention all these particulars because the reader will then recognize that since I also got a long view, a long sloping-down view of the wood and further woods beyond, seeing nothing but trees, and having behind me and at each side nothing but trees, I was in a highly favourable position, indeed a position in which not only happy hours but inspired and fruitful hours might be spent.

During the late spring and summer the sun fell upon this spot between 8 a.m. and 10 a.m. And as this was between six and eight normal time, the temperature of the sunlight could not have been improved upon. Since my job was being done on the basis of piece-work I was in command of my own time. On beautiful mornings my ideal was to do early work on the wood and sit down here for breakfast at eight when the sun had reached the oak. I took up my position carefully; back upright; head against trunk; legs straight out, with half-empty haversack under the knees, and a dry coat or sack to sit on; arms folded or hands clasped between knees. *Then* I immediately forgot my body,

abandoned it—and became all spirit or soul or mind or whatever it is that sits inside us looking out of our two windows.

And now, at this point—to justify the foregoing details—I would gladly tell you what then I knew, what then I grasped. Ah, could I but do so, then would I have the power to bless and to save, even as I was saved and blessed! But I did not quite grasp it, I did not understand the Knowledge that seemed mine. As I strove, and strove again to penetrate the meaning of the glory and the promise in the scene around, and to frame into a conception something that I seemed to *know*—it eluded me, it always just drew back. Sometimes it came very close, as if it were about three feet above my head, at times almost brushing my forehead—but not coming in, and soon fading far away again. This experience of the Undeclared Announcement trembling on the verge of utterance, was imaged by Thoreau in terms of an eagle—'an eagle that suddenly comes into the field of view, suggesting great things and thrilling the beholder, as if it were bound hitherward with a message for me; but it comes no nearer, but circles and soars away growing dimmer, disappointing me, till it is lost behind a cliff or a cloud'.

Yet something was clear to me, and I will set down here one note which I took as the nearest I could get to my finding—I turn off the road, enter the wood, and sit down under the tree. The sun gleams upon everything, there is glittering and shining everywhere. A green caterpillar is lowered down by an invisible thread in front of me, and as it swings about, the sun shines through its transparency. A little distance off a spider mounts upwards on another unseen rope, as if slowly falling upwards by inverse gravitation or being drawn up by an invisible crane, while another calmly walks on the air, and yet another takes a seat upon nothing. A bush over there is glittering with raindrops, little white lanterns fastened to the lower side of twigs; but if I swing my head slightly to one side, some of those lights turn colour, becoming red and purple. A creature alights on the back of my hand: its body being in the shape of a tiny solid canoe, which has one high brown sail rather out of proportion to the boat; suddenly the sail opens into two sails using the body at the base as a hinge, and the whole thing flies away—a butterfly, like a flying flower. Then there is the ground I sit on, the tree behind me, and the trees around me, and the flowers, and the thing I can't see, the air, yet stronger as a substance than, say, an aeroplane or a liner. A general voice is given to the whole thing by the birds. Most of this is incomprehensible to me, and even if a learned man describes what is going on and how it is all done, he will not be explaining it for me. And the interesting thing about it is that it *works*. Here we have nothing but a series of the most curious kind of miraculous activities and queer appearances and extravagant shapes, but it all works in concert. One might suppose that it could possibly work for a month or so or even a year—but it does it every year, it goes on working without mishap and without running down. This in itself fills me with a great deal of confidence and some comfort. Added to this there is the general look of the place and the spirit in the atmosphere. Indeed we have all been so struck with its aspect that we have invented a word for it—beauty. I am surrounded here with law, order, and beauty, and am myself absolutely happy here. There is nothing to make me unhappy. No evil thing meets my eye, there is nothing bad here. I begin to grasp the obvious fact that this place is—perfect. And suddenly I realize where I am! I am in the Garden of Eden. I had heard about it always as a definite place in the past. There was no error in speaking of the Garden as existing, but the mistake lay in tying it down in time and place. For it still exists—all we need is the key of the gate. The first two persons in history dwelt in the Garden, it is said. But they ate of the Tree of Knowledge and had to go. That must be the truth: at the birth of consciousness we became *onlookers* and were separated from Nature, and left the Garden to create a world of our own apart from Nature. Our next step is a further extension of consciousness when we shall realize the unity of life on a higher plane of understanding. Having tasted of *that* tree of knowledge we shall enter the Garden of Eden once more, and Paradise shall be regained.

11. ODE TO THE SUN AND TO IDLENESS

It is true that at times I sought to pierce the mystery and to grasp the truth that seemed within my reach. But very often I refrained from thinking as much as possible, wishing just to receive what was given and glory in it. I certainly set myself against irrelevant thoughts, and against evil thoughts and thoughts of bitterness or annoyance concerning the outside world, which often pursued me into the wood like loathsome hounds. To think such things here would be fearful waste of time, I felt—the precious moments must not be lost. Here there was no need to think evil or to do evil, just as there was no chance of seeing evil. It was enough merely to sit in the sun.

To sit in the sun. This is still one of the greatest experiences of life for us in the West. And it is free. No millionaire can buy up the sun and sell it to us. All the inventions through all the centuries have added nothing to this gladness, nor may any frantic folly take it away. The poor deluded multitude, dungeoned and depraved by lunatics and magnates, may prefer *artificial* sunshine, but the real thing is there all the same, and cannot be taken down.

Pardon me if on this theme I speak with some slight intemperance. I am not quite normal in my love of the sun. It has always been a passion with me, I cannot call it less. To this day I remember the feeling of outrage I experienced when, in the schoolroom, on the sun shining in, the schoolmaster would get up and *draw down the blind.* I remember thinking the man must be crazy. 'Already I began to love the sun; a boy I loved the sun, Not as I since have loved him, as a pledge And surety of our earthly life', said Wordsworth, 'But for this cause, that I

had seen him lay His beauty on the morning hills.' Thus also have I loved the sun: because of his pledge, and because of his light upon the hill; but also because he transforms me—within no less than without.

Especially in March. Then the air is still chilly, but the sun is warm again—February's feeble ray is suddenly doubled, and sometimes if we can shelter from the cold wind we can get really warm. We are cold, and when the black cloud passes across, we shiver. Then the sun emerges from the silvered margin, the glowing ball comes out and blazes down upon us. At this moment I *give myself* to the experience. I close my eyes, and it is as if a warm velvet glove were laid across my face, an invisible blanket wrapped around me. We call it heat. But what is that? Am I taken in the arms of God? Everything is transformed, this is holy ground, even I am holy, my heart is purged of sin, I forgive everything, I love all things, I am lifted up; and in understanding I pass beyond all theory, all system, resting utterly content in this blessing and this sign—worshipping the sun as if it were God himself, or at least his regent chaired beside the throne.

I have said I sat in the sun, but more often I *lay* in it—sideways, head on haversack (I cannot lie on my back). As a matter of fact I often take up this position—lying sideways—when I'm intellectually stuck over something and want to concentrate. But here I often did it because I wanted to sleep. The thing was to get as tired as possible, either by going to bed late or through strenuous work, and then lie in the sun—again especially in March or April—and go to sleep. I chose some particular spot at the foot of an ash to which the sun came and at each side of which I had placed drifts. At the chosen moment I lay down, curled up, and closed my eyes while the sun shone on my face. Often a strong, chilly wind blew, but it didn't come near me, I received only the sun. Then I entered my own special, simple paradise. I was absolutely tucked away from the world—several miles in all directions from it—I was totally hidden from sight of mortal soul, and no one knew where I was nor would be coming anywhere near me. I was free from the entire turmoil of the world. I lay there, almost sinking into, melting into the earth, waiting for sleep to come and take me right down—wondering if death in reality is more than such a joyous sinking down as this. But truly now I indulged in no thoughts, no metaphysical speculations, I became little higher than an animal—and no lower. I laughed to think what a reprehensible sight I would have made to any *busy* man who came upon me there, a sloping slacker, an untoiling son of earth! But I felt no need to offer up apologies to the unreproving Beings around. Let the world outside carry on, I would say, let them dash hither and thither, let them kill one another whole-sale, let them go to hell, I'm wrapped in the embrace of Nature and filled with peace and love! And like any dog, like any savage, I lay there enjoying myself, harming no man, selling nothing, competing not at all, thinking no evil, smiled on by the sun, bent over by the trees, and softly folded in the arms of the earth.

12. BIRDS AND ANIMALS IN THE WOOD

On such occasions I became so much part of the general furniture of the wood that my presence was not noticed by bird or animal. One day I was disturbed by a loud hammering on the oak tree. It came fiom a very small bird with a large beak. Then it flew to an ash, took up a position on a dead-looking branch and began hammering again—real hard strokes of the beak, not pecking but hitting. Then up to another place, a junction of branches and out of sight, from where I heard more hammering, and then in sight again higher up—exactly as if the bird was on business as a carpenter come to test the tree and knock in a few nails where necessary. It sometimes flew up, but more often walked up. After having made a thorough examination it descended the trunk, walking down backwards the whole way, quite oblivious of Newton's law, and knocking as it went along just as if it considered the decorative lichen needed some nailing down.

I wondered why it pecked so hard, since it would surely be difficult to catch hold of an insect that way. But bird authorities say that the insect in question is well behind the rotten bark and the beak has to pierce its way there. But how then does it see the insect to be picked up? The bird was obviously a woodpecker, I thought. But no, it was a nuthatch, a near relation. For the method of descending the tree, *walking* down either backwards or head first, distinguishes it: this mode of descent is evidently reserved for the nuthatch alone. Moreover, the woodpecker is inclined to make less of a hammering noise than a rattling; once when I heard one doing its stuff it sounded like a tractor-driver changing gear badly.

I know very little about birds, and I do not attempt to sort them out at all extensively, being content to watch them fly. The centuries pass, but we are just as fascinated as ever by these creatures who don't know what it is to *fall*, but go from the top of one tree to another upon the roads of air. They must be happy up there, we feel, housed in nests on trees, and able to pass along not in an aeroplane but as an aeroplane. But no one should even superficially compare a bird with an aeroplane: to figure such a thing one would have to imagine a bird whose outspread wings have got permanently stuck, and whose beak is a propeller. Yet the aeroplane shares this with birds—that it is a lover of woods. It is strange how pilots cannot resist the temptation to swoop down low over the tree-tops. On one particular occasion, a truly enormous and dark aeroplane passed just touching the tops of the trees above me: first the sudden thundering roar, then the flashing past of the huge structure. It was so colossal, so extreme a case, that I was driven right back across the centuries and saw myself as an Early Man in the jungle startled by the miraculous appearance of a flying monster, and dashing off to join the amazed and affrighted tribe.

I have nothing new to impart about either the birds or the animals in the woods. The usual performances were gone through here in the usual way. An agonizing screech at intervals broke the sylvan utopianism as intimated by the gentle cooing of the dove: but I could never be sure whether the cry was of death or love, pain or pleasure. The sudden loud flapping of unseen wings within the shades often startled me. The cuckoo made its appearance in due course, uttering its throaty gurgle while on the wing, and its famous announcement when in the tree. Occasionally a crow flew across, not as the crow is supposed to fly, but with sudden slight turnings and sharp hesitations as if it had remembered something too late. Sometimes, though very seldom, a peewit appeared, lover not of the woods but of the field and the wide desolate place dedicated to history and slow time, into which that plaintive cry, those mournful numbers, flow and melt away.

The birds which most often—late in the year—provided me with entertainment were the starlings. An immense force had taken up residence quite close, and towards evening they carried out extensive manoeuvres. Suddenly I would hear a noise from above as if a gale were blowing up, and I would see a black cloud moving much faster than a cloud; and as it moved, this composition of birds closed to the size of a football, then opened in the shape of a fan, closed again and now became a snake a hundred yards long twirling about in the air, then a carpet being shaken by invisible hands—each transformation being carried out with great celerity. Every bird went perfectly in wing with all the rest, so that however much the gathering twisted and turned it looked more like a single strange creature than a company—the few stragglers like feathers that had been blown off the body owing to the violence of the movement. What the purpose of all these operations was, I don't know. It gave all the appearance of being without utilitarian motive, and is, ten to one, pure *joie de vivre*, play, art for art's sake.

As for animals, I very often heard a sudden nervous chortle followed by a scampering noise, and looking up saw a red or grey squirrel, the creature that always delights us by the beauty of its tail and the strength of those paws that turn the perpendicular into the flat. Immediately my dog would bark, and it would dash higher up. Yet its behaviour was curious. It was as safe as a church in those branches; but it didn't think so, and leapt frantically from tree to tree, accomplishing jumps which made me nervous, and then coming to a very wide jump, failed to make it, landed on the ground uninjured, and scuttled into the undergrowth. It could have remained at ease in the first tree it went up. The species to which it belongs has had centuries behind it of practising in thus escaping from the earthbound beasts. Why has it not learnt to stay put in the security of the lofty boughs? Why does it lose its head?

The deer had more sense in using their legs. There were quite a few of these wonderful animals in the Chase, and the barks of the trees had suffered accordingly, for deer have a partiality for the barks of young trees. I did not see very many. Occasionally when I was making no noise, one appeared and came quite close. If I remained silent and absolutely still it did not observe me. For animals do not see with their eyes. Not that they are blind; it is that objects are not individually separated by a governing intelligence. This extraordinary fact has saved many a man's life in the jungle, and made close observation of animals possible for the naturalist. Then if I stepped on a breaking twig or deliberately clapped my hands it would leap away through the wood with that aristocracy of speed and grace that makes these creatures the queens of the forest. On an early morning in the half-light at a particularly lonely part of the Chase I saw a whole drove of them, and on another occasion at the same hour my dog gave chase to a solitary deer. It stopped and gave battle, and to my astonishment it looked as if my dog was getting the best of it. I called him off. Afterwards I was sorry that I had done so, for I might have witnessed a truly jungle scene.

Some animals alarmed me rather than I them. The tiny weasel pursuing a large rabbit mesmerized to a slow wobbling gait, is a sight most monstrous and intimidating. Indeed, weasels almost paralyse me. Once I sat at a place where three holes abutted at a few feet distance from each other. When I sat down there a weasel looked out of one of

the holes and spat at me as if delivering a curse, then retired only to appear immediately at the next hole to hiss me again, after which it drew back its head and shot it out again at the third hole to curse me from that angle. This performance went on for some time: I had to keep turning my head first one way then another as each second the ferocious face looked out of a hole to glare and spit and curse. It seemed to be charged with such potency that I really wouldn't be surprised if I saw a weasel pursuing an elephant paralysed with fear.

Another creature that alarmed me was the adder. Now and then I came upon the reptile, even two or three together. In grey scales or in chequered green. Finding one of considerable size, I toed it, and it rushed away through the privet's undergrowth at extraordinary speed. It didn't crawl, squirm, or hunch its way forward; but *glided* along—as astonishing as if you saw a boat dash through the water without oars or screw. I caught it up in my hand by its middle. It turned its visored head round, opened its trap-door of a mouth, and stuck its barbed fang deep into my thick leather glove (which I had carefully slipped on). Once, twice, three times it struck, then gave up and simply kept darting in and out of its mouth that long terrible tongue, shaped at the end like a tiny anchor or arrow-head. Now and then it gave great wrenches with its whole body to escape my grasp. But I held it firmly and gazed steadfastly into its primeval countenance. It is remarkable how utterly baffling such a creature is. One gazes, one tries to concentrate, but somehow one cannot *take it in.* One can hold a conversation with a dog; one could almost shake a horse by the hoof; many a sow is as human to look at as a Victorian lady being amused; a cow often reminds us of some friends; a lamb might be a baby; the birds, like many of us, are vocalists; the monkey shares our secret. But the reptile—I'm afraid no communication is possible. However, I put this one down to pursue its destiny without further hindrance from me, as I felt it had the right to do.

I shall not add much more to my list, but I loved the owl because of its astonishing silence and lightness of touch; I admired the nightjar which was like an alarm-clock which couldn't stop; and it would be wrong to forget the pheasant, little pleasure as that poor lumbering bird gives us. Every time I approached the wood it startled me by suddenly springing out of some hidden place on my path with its appalling rattle of a screech and made its straight, blundering, joyless flight away through the wood. That jarring sound is the nearest thing in Nature to something mechanical—as if a machine had been made by mistake. Which reminds me that there is one more animal entitled to a place here. Opposite my wood there was another one belonging to another estate, and rising on a slope so that I commanded a clear view of it. At a given time of the year the partridge and pheasant sportsmen appeared. As they beat their way along through the wood they uttered noises which brought them into such close relationship to the brute creation that it is proper to include them here in this short account of animal life found in the woods from time to time.

13. THE OLD WOODMAN

During some of the summer a woodman and his grandson came from an adjoining estate to make hurdles out of the hazel which I had cut down. And at last, at long last, I came upon the countryman of tradition, the countryman celebrated in books, but who can now only be found in odd corners. He was not a Hardy 'character', nor a Wordsworthian 'leech-gatherer'. Not an 'amusing' man, nor 'quaint', nor given to making 'wise' remarks culled from his years, nor in command of a picturesque phrase. Such men can be found in Ireland, and probably in Scotland and Wales. The English equivalent possesses no playboy characteristics, nor love of generalization, nor much sense of humour, nor desire to make an effect; but he is so completely sincere that any remark he does make has the advantage of being genuine.

He belonged to the generation that had started work sixty-odd years ago at the age of eleven, beginning then to make spar-gads and hurdles such as he is still making now. The passage of years might be written in financial terms: to-day spar-gads are thirty-five shillings a thousand as against eight shillings a thousand in the old days. To-day a man can make £1 per thousand spars while in the former era he got 2s. 6d.—his wages then in the ordinary way being 10s. a week as opposed to the £4 of to-day. Thus a man of that kind will have seen some material changes.

Though he was well into the seventies he did not show many signs of being an old man, age had not wearied him; the expression on his face had no sourness in it whatever; his manner of addressing his grandson was extremely pleasant; and he seemed to get on wholly without swearing. He was not a talker, but he enjoyed talking on general topics, and took your point at once (if you did not exaggerate).

He showed me how to make hurdles and spar-gads, and how to loop together the bundles—this last being almost as elaborate a process as hurdle-making itself. He himself had dealt with this wood eighteen years previously, and obliquely I tried to find out his opinion of my thinning and axe-work. He found no fault with it, in fact praised it. In another man I would probably have taken this for politeness; but I thought he really did mean it, and this gave me no small pleasure.

One day, after he had given me the figures regarding the spar-gads, I asked whether he thought the labourers were happier to-day. He replied firmly and without hesitation—'No, they are not.' He said they were not satisfied, and were less happy. He went on to say how he used to do general farm-work during the summer months and then return to the wood. He emphasized what a good time haymaking was in those days. Everyone turned out, whole families, having great tea-parties in the field: it was something everyone looked forward to, including the children. No one had to work at a desperate pace, for there were so many workers; and since there were so many workers the job was done quite as quickly as at the present day.

Such are the imponderables of progress. More wages, less jolliness, and the machines not making for less hard work but for fewer workers. The goal of life, judging by our actions, is efficiency. It is really happiness. And the great snag is that neither machines nor £ s. d. seem able to open that door.

In the old days if the agricultural labourer was not religious he was at any rate superstitious. The superstitious man is profounder than the blasé sceptic, for he is at least *aware* of the 'mystery', and it is one of the little ironies of life that the latter imagines himself superior. To-day the attendance at a village church is often only three. For the most part people simply do what is 'done', regardless of conviction. In the old days it was not done not to go to church. To-day it is hardly done to go. There is no superstition, and the attitude towards religion is one of indifference at best, and at worst, and most often, of undisguised derision. Hence—quite apart from *believing* this or that—the whole background of word-music from the Bible with its accompanying attitude of reverence and its sanctification of joy and sorrow, no longer informs the life of the people.

The old woodman did not belong to the generation that had lost these good things, and I knew it was safe to make a remark to him concerning the anti-religious trend of workers in general to-day. It pleased him, for presently he came out with a generalization of his own without any prompting from me. He glanced round the wood, and slowly and haltingly choosing his words, said: 'If I do say to a farmer now, Look how they plants do grow; look at thik field or yourn and see how they do grow without help; there must be a wonderful God behind they plants—he would not understand I.'

'No,' I replied, 'he would probably say that his overhead charges had been very heavy this year, and that he was not going to make nothing out of it, not a penny.'

'That's just what he would say,' affirmed the old man.

And I told him how the foreman had looked over the wood and declared—'It's only dead money.'

'Oo ah!' said the old man, 'that's the way it is now. That's the way it is.'

Not more than a month or two had passed before he and his grandson had constructed about £40 worth of hurdles. There was something extraordinarily satisfactory about the rows of them leaning neatly one against another, or staked flat ten or more feet high—all twisted by the finger of man out of the hazel-bushes, while those same bushes were engaged in sending forth new shoots for future hurdles.

It was interesting to notice how woodmen, working within a given radius for a fair length of time, generally build a comfortable shelter for themselves, against weather and as a dining-room. A few pieces of corrugated tin, two or three poles, and some straw sheaves make an excellent little room to retire into when it pours, and a cloak-room and bicycle-shed at all times. Outside the shelter, on raw winter days, a fire is lit and kept going—very pleasant at meal times. In this, as in some other respects, the woodman has the advantage over other workmen on the land. I have yet to meet the woodman willing to change his job for any other department of agricultural activity.

One day I asked the old man—'Do you ever wish that you had done anything else in life, been anything else?' He did not need to pause and think over his answer, and then perhaps give a non-commital one. 'No,' he said firmly, 'I do not, and the longer I live the more sure I am of that.'

At last I stood beside a contented man, one with many years upon his back, who did not feel that others had got a fairer deal out of life; who was not greedy for position, nor envious of riches, nor indifferent to the beauty that is freely given to the poor in places such as this.

I had noticed that he sometimes lay down and took a nap after dinner, and I mentioned how delightful it was to lie down and sleep in the wood. He agreed with me. 'It's as if thik birds do watch e,' he said, 'and thik trees do bend over e.'

14. A WAY OF LIVING

ONE of the great advantages of a woodman's job is that in his old age if he wishes to retire on his pension, he can at the same time supplement it by peaceful and easy-going piece-work. Just such an old man came to the woods from time to time to make stakes and faggots out of my drifts. He took it easy, arriving sometime before ten and going home at about four. This filled in his day beautifully. If it came on wet he was none too pleased, for 'it don't do' he said, 'to get back too early'. But he wasn't in the least anxious about the money element. His simple needs were perfectly well met by his pension and what he made in the wood, and his days were filled pleasantly. He had a very nice cottage down in the village, free. So had the other old woodman, a delightfully placed and good cottage—for there is no sense in supposing that the countryman is always or even usually badly off in this matter as against the townsman. (And the man who talks about 'the disgraceful housing conditions of rural England' should go and have a look at an Irish village!)

Anyway, in this sphere, I found happy and contented men. Modern life is a labyrinth in which most men are lost. To find a way, a path is not easy. They had found one. Nothing elaborate about it; not the way of the Cross; not the Eightfold Path; but the way of the peasant whose *wants* are few. This gets them through, and I often think of them, I shall always think of them, as men who having escaped from all the escapisms of the modern world, were at peace. I used to visualize them sometimes when, on visits to London, I found myself again in the bus or under the ground. And when I got back amongst the trees again I

would feel the full force of the farce of modern civilization; I would see with the clear vision of hatred the foul torrent of respectable insanity that makes the majority of men inferior to monkeys, and their works in thousands and thousands of cases absurd beyond the conception of any savage.

There were times when, sitting under the oak-tree in the early morning, I felt that so much was here given that if all the millionaires of all the world came ready to do my bidding and answer my Go here or Go there, I would have nothing to say except Go away. I was in a position to use my body for a period and then my head and pen. Could I ask more than this? or seeking, find? The Rights of Man are all very well, but we shall save the social world only when we pay attention to the *needs* of men. To do hard agricultural work half the day and hard cultural work the other half—that for many would answer their psychological needs. But no effort is made to make that kind of thing possible. We imagine that everything will be all right if we all produce as many objects as possible and distribute them to everybody. We refuse to think of man's Needs and go on and on thinking only of his Rights and his Pay. Never about his psychological and physiological needs—nay, never!

I could satisfy this need here, but only on condition that the whole of Europe, the whole of North America and Canada, the British Empire, Russia, China, and Japan could be engaged in warfare instead of welfare—myself only having to attend Home Guard. But there it was, I was able to do it. And I shall not easily forget, even when the frost of age is on my head, how after a few hours' work in the morning, I had earned enough to pay my rent, and in the afternoon the grocery bill. That is something that I shall never forget! And so, for a moment adopting the role of the wise councillor, I would say to any young man, or young man and woman, ambitious only for peace and sanity—Learn the craft of Forestry, enter the woods, and happiness may yet be yours.

15. DIFFERENT MOODS IN THE WOOD

I CAN offer the above small piece of advice to anyone likely to be glad of it with a clear conscience, because any woodmen I have known always seemed to be doing well and were satisfied. But, speaking very personally, given the choice between permanent agricultural work of a general nature and forestry, I would not choose forestry—though doubtless I would often long to get back to the woods again. In this account I celebrate the pleasures of working in the wood, indeed I sing its joys. But too much hangs on the weather and the time of year. Long hours in a wood during wet or dark or heavy days, can be most melancholy. One can be elated amongst trees, even inspired again and again, in conditions such as I have already rehearsed. It is also possible, and indeed a frequent experience, to be numbed by trees. On dreary, drizzly days I often became stupefied and paralysed in mind as well as weary and lifeless in body.

I have always loved to have a View. The mountains and the sea appeal to me so strongly that I do not dare to think about them nor to mark the absence in England, save in the north, of the glen, the real glen through which the river roars. Thus I'm afraid that I am quite capable of feeling too enclosed working for long periods in an English wood. I love a view, I say, even from the field on the highest part of a farm, and to plough such a field is better than any work in the wood. Sometimes when I walked through the Chase beyond my fence, wandering along, getting lost even and wondering where I had got to, and suddenly came upon a gate leading into a cornfield washing knee-deep against the cliff of trees, I felt a great nostalgia for open spaces and clear views and the turned furrow and the glorious plough.

Thus my moods would go up and down, and as I have no axe to grind save my steel one, but only truth to tell, I shall not pretend that as a woodman I could ever be wholly satisfied. My spirits were very much influenced by the weather. In the fields, the cold, the dark, the dreary, or even the wet days make much less difference, sometimes none at all, sometimes a pleasant change. But the change from sunlight to a drizzle in the wood is a very definite thing, and makes its full effect. The kingdom of heaven is within you, it is said. No doubt there is great truth in that. But an honest man must acknowledge how often his interior is dictated by the exterior scene. Sometimes I have almost felt my heart *contract* at the sudden coming on of a cold darkness, and expand at the smiling beams swiftly pervading the weary, dripping scene around.

During March, April, and May the wood is the place. The sleeping trees awake. At their feet the flowers rise up and we gaze at them with absurd surprise. The birds declaim rather than sing. We stand in the midst of rejoicing life. By June the more obvious flowers have completed their act, they have had *their* summer, their autumn, and now are in their winter of desolation. Others are taking their place—the rock-rose, the herb-willow, the garlic, the foxglove—but the abundance has gone, and the colour blue, so rich, so varied, is seen no more save in the sky. We have become accustomed to the green of the trees. The birds are reticent.

In July a hush falls upon everything. The silence is disquieting. The silence of a wood at all times is something to reckon with; it seems to pervade one's personality, and I seldom open my lips even to speak to my dog. In July it is a principality. In such an atmosphere ambition wilts, mental strife seems futile, the arts unreal. Filled with unease, one would gladly leave the silent and too solemn trees for a more human scene.

For a more deadly silence go to a pine wood. One day in June when I had wandered farther into the Chase I came to a pine plantation. I stepped out of the privet-choked pathway into its darkness. I walked there without making the slightest noise, for there is no floor, no man-made carpet so soft and yielding to the tread as these massed needles. There was not a speck of green on this ground. I felt awe in the silence. No bird sang, nor wing flapped, nor rabbit scuttled, nor stick cracked. I was enclosed and submerged in a silence like a substance. It was broken occasionally by a squall of wind heard above in the branches of the pines, that wild, watery, bare-beached, oceanic sound that even at the height of summer has no summer in it, and beats against the heart and calls to mind man's endless tale of tempest and of wrong.

Standing there in the darkness of this fir wood, I looked towards the edge and saw the greenery beyond. It had become a bright green light and I thought the sun must have come out. Yet the sun had not come out, the sky was very cloudy. But from in there that undergrowth immediately outside did shine strongly like a green light. Also in the middle of this plantation there was a pool of green—owing to a break in the trees. Where the light could penetrate, the green had formed—chiefly moss and dog's mercury, a little pool that stopped immediately at the end of the open space.

I was hardly wrong, I reflected, in imagining that I was looking out upon green lights. For that is what I was looking at. The light from heaven shone upon the ground and the plants received it, and—by virtue of chlorophyll, we say—turned it into green substance. That undergrowth is light made visible: it is light made tangible.

Cheered by the thought of this radiant miracle, I emerged from the shade of the sombre aisles and pushed my way home through the tangible pieces of sunshine that blocked my path.

16. THE SCAVENGERS OF CORRUPTION

One day in July I was cutting down a very large and thick-stemmed hazel-bush. It had been left alone for so many years that the stool was full of holes and cups and soft, dry-leaved hiding-places. I had cut away about a dozen of the branches and had lifted my axe to strike another, when my eye was caught by something in one of those recesses of the stool. Five small yellow flowers, fresh and strange, stood erect amidst a little bed of dry leaves. They quivered as if blown gently by a breeze. But there was no breeze: and looking closer I saw that they were not flowers; they were five wide open beaks of new-born birds.

Abandoning my axe I knelt down and peered into this nest thus placed so low. The beaks closed and I saw simply the creatures, sightless, no eyes yet opened, no feathers to cover them save here and there a patch of furry stuff on the red flesh. They could not see but they could hear, and when I made a noise all the beaks opened wide again, quivering and giving the impression that they were really shouting an appeal for food, though their voices could not reach me. Then their beaks closed and the pitiful, hideous little bodies sank down into the nest once more. Pathetic beyond measure. Fatally forced into Being. Trembling symbols of the sheer affliction of life, the pure burden of birth.

Those open beaks had looked like flowers for a moment. Yet how different is a flower from an animal in the matter of food. The beaks shouted in mute agonizing appeal for one thing only—the death of another that they might live. Here in this tiny nook in England, as in the roughest jungles of the world, the Law must be fulfilled—thy life

from the parent body, the polyp continues to remain attached. But it proceeds in the same way as the hydra, each polyp budding its children rather than laying or delivering them, and they all feed from the communal sac, the continual growth of which means the spreading out and up of their domicile, their polypary. This polyp, or 'coral insect', is a little hollow globule of gelatinous matter, a tiny sac whose mouth is bordered by eight leaf-shaped appendages, fringed at the edges: eight tentacles opening like the petals of a flower. No wonder a coral looks like a rock covered with brilliant flowers. What is that rock made of? How did these flower-like animals called polyps come to have this pedestal? Because it is made of their own exudations. They exude stone. With their own excrement they build up and rest upon a monument as hard as marble. The whole reef is made of polyp. The softest of all creatures has turned into the hardest of all rocks. These reefs continue to grow by means of the collective effort of millions upon milliards of polyps, so that an archipelago such as the Maldive in the Indian Ocean can comprise no less than twelve thousand reefs, and a reef can spread over an area of thirty-three thousand miles. No term needs to be set to the life of a polypary since it is a collection of beings continuously giving birth to others by process of budding, and continuously bequeathing their excrement to the magnificent ocean-dunghill upon which they stand.

All life is related by the work of the twin sisters Time and Motion—often called Evolution—and it is not hard to see how similar is the growth of a plant to the growth of a coral reef. We can see that a tree is a community of beings rather than an individual. You cannot cut limbs off an individual and expect it to live, or the limb itself to live. That is exactly what we can do with a tree. If we want a fresh tree it is sufficient to cut off a living branch and plant it. It will spread roots and grow, while the parent will not suffer. We can even plant the young branches of one tree onto another tree, which we call grafting, an operation which explains the justice of Dupont de Nemours's definition—'A plant is a family, a republic, a sort of living hive, whose inhabitants are fed in the common refectory upon the common stock of food.' This communal stock of food, this sort of omnibus sac, called the trunk, is even ready to feed a species of tree not absolutely fraternal. Figs will not grow on thistles—(though under this ruling one would not be surprised if they did). But Fabre mentions a certain pear-tree 'on which, by means of grafting, the whole gamut of cultivated pears was represented. Sweet or sour, dry or juicy, large or small, green or brilliantly coloured, all these pears ripened on the same tree, year after year, always unchanged, faithful to the racial characteristics, not of the tree, their foster-mother, but of the various buds transferred to this common support'. Such an experiment might well have served as a proof of the individuality of a bud as opposed to the free association of a tree.

This granted, the age of a tree could be very great. In fact if it lives in a spot unexposed to the violence of storm or earthquake and out of the reach of man's commercial activity, it may continue to live for an extraordinary period. A good place to find tree-veterans is in the sanctified area of graveyards where, companions of the dead, they are unmolested by the living. Thus in the cemetery of Allouville in Normandy there stands an oak-tree some nine hundred years old, whose trunk at ground level shows a circumference of thirty-three feet, while within the aerial forest of its upper branches the cell of an anchorite has been built, and the lower portion of its partly hollow trunk has been used since 1696 as a chapel dedicated to our Lady of Peace. Many a yew-tree in an old churchyard vies in age with the most ancient church, while others look back to times long before any temple was built in the name of Christ. There was a yew-tree at Fortingal in Scotland whose concentric rings amounted to two thousand five hundred, and another at Brabourne in Kent whose age was thirty centuries. Oak-trees often stand sturdily against the blasts of time. In 1824, a woodcutter in the Ardennes, on felling a giant of this species, found fragments of sacrificial urns and ancient medals within its trunk, thus connecting it with the barbarian invasions of Europe. It showed no more signs of failing health than the walnut-tree noticed by the soldiers of Balaclava in the Crimea, which, though two thousand years old, yielded an annual crop of 100,000 walnuts, the harvesting of which was shared by five families.

The size of such trees can best be imagined when we learn that on the occasion of a giant conifer which once stood on the slopes of the Sierra Nevada in California, falling before the axe, the woodmen had to use a long ladder even to mount its prostrate trunk, as if scaling the roof of a house. The bark of this tree was removed in a single piece from a length of twenty-two feet, which served to enclose a room in which one hundred and forty children could play hunt-the-slipper. This giant displayed three thousand concentric layers of wood, showing that it reached back to the time when, according to tradition, 'Samson released in the cornfields of the Philistines, foxes, to whose tails incendiary torches were attached'. These conifers of the Sierra Nevada had grown to three hundred feet or more. Other veterans have expressed themselves more in their crowns, like that yew-tree in the cemetery of Haie-de-Routot which in 1832 spread its foliage over the entire churchyard and part of the church itself. I have already mentioned the Chestnut Tree of the Hundred Horses at Etna, under the cover of which the Queen of Aragon found room for her whole retinue; but in Mexico there is a cypress contemporary with Noah, standing in the cemetery of Santa Maria de Fesla near Oaxaca, beneath whose boughs, Cortez, the conqueror of Mexico, found room to shelter his army. The crown of the baobab-tree at Senegambia near Cape Verde, is even more remarkable. The diameter of the trunk is greater than the height of the tree, the latter being but fifteen feet and the former thirty!—a column fit to support the mighty dome which is two hundred feet in diameter. This baobab-tree is a worthy companion in distinction with the dragon-tree of Orotova in the Canary Islands whose trunk cannot be encircled by ten men holding hands. Both trees, older than the Pyramids, hold the memory of six thousand years, and show every promise of ignoring the terms of Time.

18. THE FEELING INTELLECT

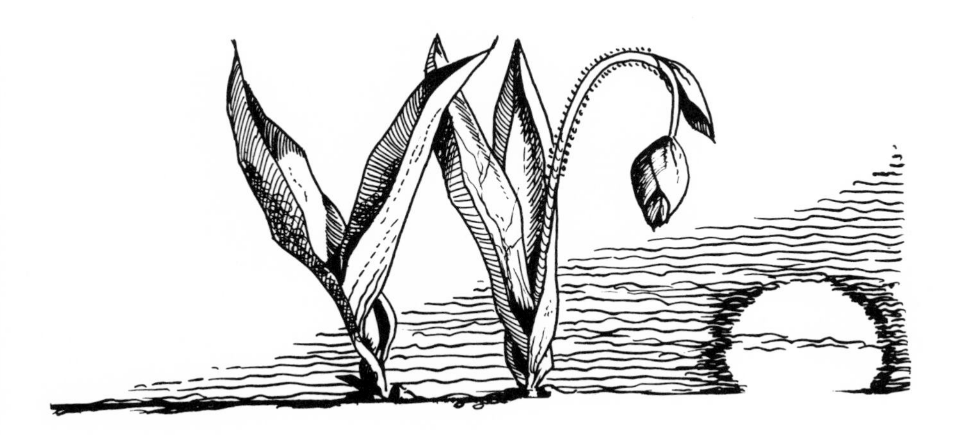

On sultry summer days it was interesting to observe the insectitude activity. Before the temperature rose the air would be moderately clear, but when the sun came out into the heavy, windless, sultry atmosphere then swarms of insects, especially a certain kind of fly, rising from nowhere particular, began to buzz round and round madly as if at that moment created, released, unloosened from a melting solid.

A massive, solid unity—that's the impression one often gets of the earth; almost motionless and asleep at the freezing Poles, partially melted into bits at these climes, and in the Tropics, under the equatorial rays, melted out into a seething flow and flood of fast-moving particles in every shape and size.

Why does life hang together so well, seeing that everything is at everything else's throat? Presumably because it is not really in parts. It is not a question of parts that make a whole but of a whole presenting itself in parts. If this were not so, the parts would certainly not hang together, they would hang separately as it were. The unity is so obvious that it would hardly seem worth mentioning; yet I cannot feel any confidence that the reader will regard it as a platitude. Certainly our *working-habit* of thought is not unity, not synthesis; it is almost always in terms of disunity, which, so far from being regretted has been conceived as excellent, as a triumph meriting the title of 'victorious analysis'. The results are not wholly good. We can do wonders with the inorganic—there we are victorious, able to create a thing like the gramophone no less than other mechanical constructions, not all of which are beautiful or of good report. But in the field of medicine (not surgery), of religion, of philosophy, of economics and politics, we are nearly lost—because we cannot yet think in terms of the unity. (We do better in the field of agriculture, because we have to act in terms of unity or perish.)

I enter thoughts of this kind in this account because they arise when I am confronted with Nature. If thoughts are simple experience arising from common sensation, they are sometimes worth putting down. I hope I have Reason on my page. But not ratiocination, not thinking before I experience. It is Wordsworth's '*feeling* intellect' that holds interest for me. The old adage 'I think, therefore I am' is less helpful than the other way round, 'I am', that is 'I experience, therefore I think'. Wordsworth held that ecstasy is the highest form of thought, since it is the nearest we get to *communication* with truth. And after a visitation of ecstasy caused in him by the earthly spectacle, he said—'Thought was not, *in enjoyment it expired*'.

If it be complained that on this showing our systems simply follow our feelings I see no harm in it. Sensation is not so very eccentric. We back each other up. Anyway, to think without the thought springing from felt experience cannot but be as void as merely second-hand thinking—with which anyone could fill a book, and which is as valueless as second-hand observation. During the daily intercourse of life we need second-hand thinking all the time, but if we do not experience our own philosophy and religion we have none. And if we write it down we do not expect to be able to hand it to anyone else. This kind of knowledge 'cannot be handed from one person having it to another person not having it', as Whitman said. But we can support the findings of others, and stimulate experience-knowledge.

The love of Nature is deep in England. And I think that what is behind this love is the instinct that Nature has a secret for us, and answers our questions. Take that foxglove over there—for we have now reached August in this chronicle. It stands singly where there had been such a wonderful display of bluebells that it then looked as if a section of the sky had been established upon earth (though not really the same colour at all!). That foxglove with its series of petal-made thimbles held up for sale to the bees, puts me at ease upon the subject of—progress. It is quite obvious that the foxglove cannot be *improved.* There is no progressing beyond that point for that particular Appearance. There is no room for improvement in the bluebell nor in any of the other exhibits. The fact is we get perfection in this form and in that form. Hence Shakespeare's 'ripeness is all', and Tennyson's 'God fulfils Himself in many ways', and Whitman's 'there can never be any more perfection than there is now', and Heraclitus' 'Life is a Fountain of Fire, an ever-living Flame, kindled in due measure, and in like measure extinguished'. Evolution is not something going up and up and up—but a series of perfect Forms. The goal of each Form is the fulfilment of its own unique perfection. There is no point in our gazing raptly into the future for paradise if it is at our feet.

But this is not true of Man, you say. That is the paradox. In a perfect world he is imperfect. But then he has attained a new thing of his own—consciousness. Complete consciousness will be his ripeness, his perfection. That will probably take time, say several million years. But why worry? there might be five million years after that of perfect humanity. Meanwhile our foxglove can keep us sane at least about subjects such as beauty and art. There is no steady evolutionary 'progress' in these things, only different expressions. Just as there will never be a better foxglove so there will never be a better Shakespeare.

Near the foxglove are the bluebells. They have now dried into seeds. Every stalk is hung with a rattling belfry of seed pouches. These once green stalks are now dry, yellow, and very light. Each bell is a hard, closed pouch of seed. I pluck a whole stalk and open one of the pouches. I find an average of fifty seeds in each, and on each stalk there is an average of eight pouches. $8 \times 50 = 400$. There are ten stalks in every area of, say, my boots' width and length—that is, room for 4,000 seeds. Looking round, one is impressed by the massive number of possible bluebells. It is impossible not to feel the sweep of Nature's vitality. What is plainly seen is not death, but everlasting creation and life. Such a scene is as much a revelation as the early garment of blue, it is as truly a sign of goodwill, and has in it as great a promise. There is no need to *reconcile* oneself to the scene. A very small proportion of those seeds will succeed in their struggle for birth, and after birth not all will succeed in getting up. But what of it? It's worth the candle, isn't it? It is better than a *void*, surely. But if the Beginner of life could do what He has done, why could He not have done better, it may be complained; why could He not have eliminated the seamy side? Evidently He couldn't.

19. EACH ITS HOUR

In the woods, as elsewhere, it is generally wrong to suppose that we often get the beginning of autumn in September, either in terms of temperature or colouring. I noticed no marked difference in the wood from what it was in the earlier month except that nothing now was due to have its hour. I have often used that phrase to myself, 'have its hour', with regard to woodland scenes; for it is interesting the way in which nearly everything has its particular hour when it, and perhaps it alone, catches the eye of the careless passer-by, though before that time, and again after it, there is nothing strikingly noticeable in that quarter.

Take the elder, for example. There, surely, is a miserable affair; a hopelessly plebeian plant. A bush posing as a tree, a tree failing to be a bush. It is impossible to praise its bark even when healthy, and when in decay it is an inch-thick pole of dirt, the nearest thing to real dirt to be found in Nature. Yet during a few weeks in July the elder has its hour. You actually pause to admire it. For then it is in flower; and those flowers are handed to you on a plate, as it were, or rather they are plates, beautifully decorated with the finest lace, held up before you. The same is true of the hawthorn. During the winter you hardly look at it, not to mention the unfriendly aspect of all armoured trees; but in spring first come the little round white buttons, and then the open flower turning half the tree to white against the blue sky, and giving out that scent which pronounces the spring and comes across to us less like a scent than a memory and a promise of happiness. More spectacular, though less rich, is the hour of that other bush the blackthorn, which, being neglected through the months, as it were, seizes upon our attention in March by a special act—that of jumping the season of green and going straight to the flower, white first and green second: so that all eyes are drawn towards this one illumination. For at this time there is no green on bush or tree in all the countryside; only the fields are green—and then how lovely they look in their brown and almost black frames! Ah, then it is that the green fields of England shine. All else is dark, but they are light. Then suddenly the darkest of all the hedges are lit by artificial snow, the blackthorn becomes the whitethorn, and the poor bush that was so humble is exalted, and its proud peers rebuked.

Speaking as a woodman, I am no friend of the privet; for not only is it very difficult to clean up, but it strays and straddles about without beauty to recommend it; but I am not blind to the fact that in July it also comes into its own and looks positively pretty. Still less do I care for the honeysuckle; but I cannot deny that when those pieces of 'twine' show the green leaf and then the flower, they become the opium of the woods.

Life being what it is, we cannot say that everything has its great hour, though all have their hours of youth, even the evergreens, which though green for ever, put up new leaves every year. And some have two hours: the most striking example being the larch which is seen, when you survey from a rise some stretch of woodland still unleafed, to be the exception—a deep rich meadow-green amidst all the surrounding unopened twigs: and again in autumn it is often so fantastically striking in its decay that that which was dead seems alive again. The imperious hours of the laburnum, lilac, and chestnut need no recommendation from me; but the whitebeam holds our attention almost more than any of the others in spring when the grey sheen of the underleaf shines out, and later when in flower the whole tree is one of the aristocrats of the forest.

Some trees prefer to take their hour in winter. I would put in a claim here for the oak, though possibly its real moment is in spring when in fresh leaf it out-greens everything else—even the beech. But there can be no two opinions that the plane-trees come into their own properly in winter when they hold up their little balls before the gaze of the Londoner. And the same is the tale of the elm. It is a question of tracery. The tracery of plane-trees and elms is scripture. Could we read that writing, we feel we would have our answer, we would solve our problem, and be shielded from the dark sorrows of our weakness.

It is the elm that knows how to take the sunset better than any other tree. I have been made to pause in my path many a time by elm-tree tracery hung across the dusky winter sky. As I write these words, I recall, so clearly, how having gone up the stairs to the top floor of a high building at Rugby School, I stopped in the passage leading to the class-room. From the window I could see a marvellous sunset behind a line of elm-trees. I stood there for some time fixed by the sight. I came in late to that lesson and may have been reprimanded, I don't remember. Nor do I remember the lesson that day, nor the master, though I think it was G. F. Bradby. But now recalling that hour, I venture to praise the boy, who must have been capable of learning something from the stolen tuition, otherwise he would not have paused to take it. The child is father to the man, we say. Let me then praise my father, even salute him: for he stood there without any ulterior motive, furtively gazing into heaven: he didn't make a song about it, didn't dream of writing it up as a poem to be praised and admired—just stood and gaped!

20. PLANTING; THE HEAD WOODMAN; THE FABLE

DURING the autumn I did some planting. My thinning process left plenty of room for useful underplanting. There are certain trees which grow best in their early years under shade, and amongst these are beech. Rolf decided to underplant the section of the wood that had been thinned, with beech. There had been a good deal of rain in September and thus the ground was all right for planting in October.

I have just been looking through two forestry manuals to find out what they said regarding Season for Planting. They said nothing. They talked about everything else. So I turned to William Cobbett's manual, not thinking it likely that *he* would let me down. Nor did he. He says with his usual dogmatic clarity—'If the weather be open and dry, you *may* plant at any time between September and April.' He then goes on to explain which are the very best times. I was interested to note that he says you should not plant in the rain, for I had often heard it so plausibly asserted that it was splendid to plant in the rain, since you are *watering* the roots as you plant. 'A grand day for planting', said a forester to me one wet afternoon, adding how he had already planted five hundred trees that day. As he happened to be a particularly glib, plausible man, I was not a bit surprised to be faced with a totally opposite school of thought on the subject—'Never plant in *wet* weather, nor when *the ground is wet*, if you can possibly avoid it,' says Cobbett again (as you see from the italics). 'The ground never *ought* to be either moved, or walked upon, when it is wet at the top. But we are frequently compelled to do both, or to leave our work wholly undone. It is a very great error to suppose that plants take root quicker for being planted in wet weather. The contrary is the fact. One great thing is, to make the earth that goes close to the roots *fine*; and this you cannot do in wet weather. For this reason it is that I prefer March and April for doing the work of planting: but, be it done at what season of the year it may, the ground ought *not to be wet*; for then it falls in about the roots in lumps, or in a sort of flakes, like mortar. It never gets close and compact about the roots; and if you tread it in it becomes, in dry weather, so hard as to actually pen up the roots of the tree as if they were in a vice.'

We did not plant in the rain, but we did plant in the autumn, for circumstances were such as to permit it, the head woodman being able to come along at that time with two boys and another woodman. This headman, whose name was Reggie Wyman, was not the same type as the woodman previously alluded to. He was only thirty-five, thus belonging to this generation, though not the last lap of it. If the new generation were composed of men like him (and there may be many such), then we need not feel too gloomy about the future. He hadn't the rather over-serious virtues of the older race, but he had his own virtues, chief of which was—humanness. The great thing is to find a human being; that is, a person capable of friendship and affection, and not submerged beneath class-consciousness, or envy, or disappointment, or frustration, or general grudgingness—and possessing life and inner warmth. We are never markedly successful in our search in any quarter. As the working man emerged from his long helotism, his attitude towards the world was inevitably often obstructively self-defensive. Now it becomes unnecessary, while dignity and pride, unforced, are often substituted. Reggie was in possession of inner warmth, and he felt in no sense inferior to anyone anywhere (but *not* the 'I'm-as-good-as-you' attitude), nor his work of less value and importance to society than the highest in the land. He was too proud and too conscious of this; but in him even that was delightful. For one's attitude towards a man, and his own attitude towards life for that matter, depends so much upon his personality—(history is governed nearly as much by this as by economic factors). Reggie had considerable personality, and of an attractive kind. Most working men look older than their arithmetical age. He looked younger. The most striking attribute of his slight wiry figure with its good-looking bronzed face, was his hair—a crop of apparently not-thinning, silky flaxen hair. Always conscious of his appearance, he never wore a hat or cap—again rare amongst working men. He fitted perfectly into the woodland surroundings, as he stood leaning against a tree—he was then the best-dressed man, in his 'shabby' workman's clothes, that I have seen in the course of my life. Realizing this, he frequently draped himself against a tree while gossiping in his high-pitched voice.

He brought with him for this planting, three assistants—an old man and two boys. Boys, as is well known, 'have no character', so one can just say boys and be done with it, recognizing that the word boy denotes life as yet unquenched or tamed; and that the extraneous wrappings of our barbarian modernism, like any other garment, could be exchanged in a twinkling if and when there are leaders of the people ready to introduce new values. Over against these boys was the old man, small, faded, insignificant, and incredibly inoffensive and humble, with nothing to say and hardly ever saying anything—he just wanly smiled amiably.

The method of planting is straightforward enough. You take a spade and thrust it into the soil at a perpendicular angle, and then at right angles to the cut you strike across it: finally dig in again at the foot of the cross, and tilt the spade backwards—and there will be a hole in the centre into which you can place your plant. The main thing is to get it properly in, with its roots spread out and not bunched together—to which end it is good to pull it up a fraction at the last moment while you take away the spade and tread down the earth firmly around the little tree.

Taking a line each, we proceeded to underplant with beech-trees a given acreage of the thinned ash-wood. Reggie worked by fits and starts, urging the boys forward in his high voice for a period, after which he often paused for a gossip. Keen on music-hall, he would outline the merits of various comedians, then get down to some more planting before pausing again, to admit, perhaps, that he couldn't do with B.B.C. talks or classical music—which latter he described as 'music which stops and then goes on again'. The Announcers also intrigued him, and he referred to a Yorkshire one who was at that time being tried out, as sounding 'rather common'—though this did not mean that he liked Stuart Hibberd, whom actually he couldn't understand, could not *follow*. Then some more planting followed by a further extension of gossip, this time on the characteristics of a certain foreman of the estate, who had once, but once only, attempted to interfere in the affairs of the wood, and of that man's 'ignorance'—i.e. manners—when he called at Reggie's house and looked his wife up and down. More planting, and then likely enough a brief outline of the moral life of the village owing to the influx of the military when too many girls became a soldier's relaxation. His tone on most matters was the normal one of cheerful scorn, but on this latter he was rather scandalized, for, though not in the least religious, he was very moral, and a great family man, in love with his wife and daughter, proud of the way his daughter had him under her thumb and highly indignant with Beveridge for presuming to extend State Assistance towards her upkeep, for he could look after his own maid, thank you, he didn't want no state assistance for his little maid. . . . And thus between our spurts of planting we covered a good deal of ground in conversation. But I write these lines in sadness, for not then did I guess, nor he in any faint way glimpse, the tragedy close ahead that would shatter him.

I do not remember how many trees we planted per day. Not too many I hope—for I want to come and watch this wood from time to time. This is a job which, were I owner, I would not like to have had done in a hurry, and might even feel inclined to praise the man who had planted the least trees per day. Certainly it would be fatal to have it done by piece-workers.

It is said—is it not?—that some men have a special 'touch' when planting, and that the trees put in by them thrive better than others. Hardy represents Giles Winterborne as such. One enjoys that sort of statement, and swallows it. But we may well doubt whether it is really ever actually true. It would be interesting to adopt a severe scientific scepticism towards it and put it to the proof over a given number of acres for a given period of years (that is the scientific method) and see at the end if the magic-touch man really did better than Tom, Dick, and Harry, when they planted properly. Actually I asked the older men whether there was anything in this, and they didn't see what I was getting at. That's always my difficulty—the meeting in real life an approximation to fictitious characters. Take another assertion from Thomas Hardy (no man loves re-reading him more than I), when he says of his woodlanders—'From the light lashing of the twigs upon their faces when brushing through them in the dark, they could pronounce upon the species of the trees whence they stretched; from the quality of the wind's murmur through a bough, they could in like manner name its sort afar off.' I did not strike lucky in coming across woodmen here, old or young, who would answer to that, any more than to Giles's capacity to make a generalization such as 'She's been a bit of a charmer in her time, I believe, a body who has smiled where she has not loved, and loved where she has not married'.

Having planted our acreage, we fenced it in, since everything being food for something else, young barks are much appreciated by rabbits. But our fence was not high enough to keep out deer. I should add here that besides my thinning and planting I carried out systematic pruning over one portion of the wood. There are, of course, two schools of thought concerning the advisability of pruning trees—that is taking away all branches as high as you can reach in order to ensure a straight, thick pole. Since I did prune a portion I shall be able to compare results. Knocking away the rotten lower branches, is not the same thing as pruning and is called 'brashing'. This is a very enjoyable job when dealing with the fir variety of tree, for then a single slash with the back of the bill-hook knocks off a number of branches with a loud bang, and you get a clear space. A few more whacks and you see the straight trunk hitherto completely hidden by the multitude of small branches.

Though I planted, thinned, pruned, and brashed I took no part in the final operation of felling. This takes place when the tree has reached 'maturity'. Sometimes, at this stage trees look so well that owners have felt constrained to leave them standing. This is deplorable. It betrays uncertainty as to the purpose of life, which is commerce. We should always bear in mind the noble words of Mr. C. E. Curtis who in his *Practical Forestry* writes—'If we visit woods in any part of the country we see this—(trees which having attained maturity have not been touched)—and with regret, and attribute it either to ignorance or to love of the scenic rather than the commercial aspect of forestry on the part of the landowner.'

Joking apart, if a man does not cut down his trees at the proper time, it really means that he does not take the job seriously. That has been the case in England far too long. People want quick returns, and nothing is less quick than the returns of forestry—though if the whole thing is planned systematically there is a splendid ultimate return and *continuous* takings the whole time on faggots, firewood, stakes, spars, poles, fencing material, shaws, and hurdles. Unfortunately the general attitude towards planting trees is a feeling that only after one is dead will the rewards be coming in. We are reminded of Dr. Johnson's saying—'Most men when exhorted to plant a tree begin *to think of dying*.' They are discouraged by the thought that they shall not live to see the pecuniary profit of their endeavour. A sad reflection, which only serves to make out a case for State Ownership in order to arrest the decay of British Forestry. Yet any man who is in a position to go in for it, is with absolute certainty carrying out noble work, supplying the material for countless things necessary to the life of mankind, work which also has a moral and beautiful aspect. Cobbett, who saw much profit in the business, proving it with facts and figures for his day at any rate, also reminds us of La Fontaine's fable of *The Old Man And The Three Young Men*—'the wise, the generous, the noble sentiments of which ought to be implanted in every human breast . . . I beg those, who may happen not to understand French, to be pleased to receive, from my pen, the following statement of the mere prosaic meaning of these words of this absolutely inimitable writer, who, in marks of simplicity the most pleasing that ever followed the movements of a pen, has, on numerous subjects, left, to ages unborn, philosophy the most profound and sentiments the most just and exalted.' After which inimitable introduction Cobbett gives the following translation of La Fontaine's fable.

> A man of fourscore was planting trees. 'To *build* might pass; but to *plant* at such an age!' exclaimed THREE YOUNG MEN of the neighbourhood. 'Surely,' said they, 'you are doting; for in God's name, what *reward* can you receive for this, unless you are to live as long as one of the Patriarchs? What good can there be in loading your life with cares about a time you are never destined to see? Pray devote the rest of your life to thoughts on your past errors; give up distant and grand expectations: these become only us YOUNG MEN.' 'They become not even you,' answered the OLD MAN. 'All we do comes late and is quickly gone. The pale hand of fate sports equally with your days and with mine. The shortness of our lives puts us all on a level. Who can say which of us shall last behold the light of heaven? Can any moment of your lives even secure you a second moment? My great-grandchildren will owe shady groves to me: And do you blame me for providing delight for others! Why, the thought of this is, itself, a *reward* which I *already* enjoy; I may enjoy it tomorrow and for some days after that; nay, I may more than once even see the sun rise on your graves.' The OLD MAN was right: one of the three, ambitious to see the New World, was drowned in the port; another pursuing fame in the service of Mars, was suddenly stopped by an unexpected shot; the third fell from a tree, on which he himself was putting a graff: and the OLD MAN, lamenting their sad end, engraved on their tomb the story here related.

21. EXPERIMENTS AND QUESTIONS

'Leaf by leaf crumbles the gorgeous year' wrote the poet. But sometimes the year really *falls*, comes crashing down. Thus here, in November when the leaves were ready to fall but had not done so owing to lack of wind, there suddenly came a tempest lasting a day and a night. Next morning I looked round in vain for leaves still at their stations and saw only one, the terminal leaf on the highest branch of a young hazel-bush: just that one, a battered flag that had not fallen. Immediately I stepped into winter.

There are not many beautiful autumn trees, when you come to think of it: not many, I mean, that amaze us like the terrific screens of beech leaves, the bright yellow of chestnut-trees, the workmanship put into the evening drapery of the larch and silver birch. These do amaze us however often we see the show; we never look on them with indifference: that the decay of the leaf should be the glory of the leaf, that its day of withering and downfall should rival the beauty of its first unfolding, is a perennial encouragement to all mankind. I do not make any great claim for the ash as a particularly good autumn tree, I think it takes the winter best; but no tree at this time of year displays a more fascinating scheme of seeds—the famous 'bunch of keys' inaptly called.

At this point I must quote Cobbett again (it is always a job to refrain from quoting him if he has touched upon a matter in hand, but I do my best to refrain, recognizing that it is my business unfortunately to give you Collis and not Cobbett). 'If you be curious and have a mind to see a tree in embryo', he writes, 'take an ASH seed, put it into a little water lukewarm, and there let it remain for three or four days. Take it out: take a sharp knife, split the seed longways down the middle, and there you will see, standing as upright as a dart, an ASH tree, with leaves, trunk, and stem; that is to say the head of the root: and all this you will see with the naked eye, as clearly as you ever saw an ASH tree growing in a field or meadow.'

Being extremely eager to see this I tried the experiment carefully. But I did not see it. I often tried but I never saw the little tree. Using a razor blade I slit the casket that holds the kernel, according to instructions, and I did find something. I found a very neat miniature *spade*. It was exceedingly attractive and surprising to look at, but it was not a tree.

William Cobbett is one of the most convincing writers who ever lived; even when wholly wrong, even when making a prophecy such as that the locust-tree will, in fifty years, be the most common in England (owing to his advocacy), even then he is so unqualified in the certitude of his tone that we feel that we *ought* to see locust-trees everywhere. And it may be that he was not right in this claim about the embryo ASH tree. But I am inclined to think that the fault lies with me. This sort of thing, curiously enough, is often a matter of psychology. Experiments *don't work* for me. For other men, or rather for a scientist (who is a special kind of person), the right thing happens at the right time. The great scientist—and of course we are not thinking of anyone like Cobbett—is a man to whom things *occur*. He is not only a man of great research and organization of particulars, he is a man for whom things occur. An example of how they do not occur for me might amuse a reader willing to wander for just a moment away from trees. When wishing to acquaint myself with the life and habits of earth-worms, I studied as my chief source of information Charles Darwin's book *The Formation of Vegetable Mould Through the Action of Worms,* published in 1881 by John Murray. Amongst other things, he established by careful experimental proof, how the worms manage slowly to bury objects, from stones to cities, if left alone. One day, when strolling in a great Cathedral Cloister, I observed that the grass in the middle contained many flat-slabbed tombstones, some modern, some quite ancient. How interesting, I thought, here I shall be able to see the result of worm-burial before my eyes. I saw a modern stone, 1921, how it was level with the grass, and near it another stone, 1804, which had sunk a considerable distance below the surface. This was excellent. I walked round so that I might see the old tombstones well sunk while the newer ones were still on the surface. I came to Martha Hunt, of Beloved Memory, dated 1870, and then to Nathaniel Groves, Resting in the Lord, dated 1791. But Martha Hunt's tombstone had sunk lower than that of Nathaniel Groves! Trying not to notice this, I passed on and continued to conduct my researches. Some of the other stones conformed to the requirements of the theory, but not all. Coming upon Arthur Mackensie of Beloved Memory, dated 1801, and then upon Elizabeth Wakefield, in Loving Memory of, dated 1910, I was grieved to see that the latter was lower than the former.

I need not say that I do not at all dispute Darwin's findings. Apart from the fact that a hundred reasons could doubtless be given as to why these particular stones were as they were, I feel confident that no fault lay with the worms. It is merely psychologically impossible for things of this kind to turn out well for me. Had Darwin experimented here, we can be sure that the tombstones would have arranged themselves in the proper order. The poet is the man who sees. The philosopher is the man who thinks. The man-of-action is the man who knows what to do. The scientist is the man who discovers. These are special kinds of men, as is soon found by any Tom, Dick, or Harry who assuming the role of one, attempts to see or to think or to lead or to experiment. I fear that I have nothing of the scientist in me, nothing of the naturalist or botanist; I shall never propose a theory supported by experimental proof, I shall never discover anything, never make new things known. I am content to make known things new.

Sometimes I am willing to ask a question. But not often, owing to the difficulty of getting a reply. For instance, I cannot understand why all woods are not found on the highest part of the land. Should not all woods be on hills? It is remarkable what colossal results follow upon minute and slow processes. We see this everywhere, not least in the famous case of the earth-worm; and we might well be pardoned if we failed to believe that the mighty rocks of the early world could ever, by any process however slow, have been changed into soil. Now trees are things which in winter are one size and in summer another size, for they put on clothes called leaves. In the winter a given tree may look quite small—and in the summer enormous. Just outside my window there is a particular example of this, a silver birch. In the winter its marvellous network of twigs gives it a frail look, but when it becomes enleafed the change is remarkable; by midsummer it is a towering substance, a mighty mammoth of a tree standing there in the dusk huge and monumental. In the autumn it does not retain this extra substance, it lets it all fall to the ground. And those leaves do not all evaporate, many of them become vegetable mould. How is it then that after a few years, let alone a few centuries, a forest will not have added enormously to the ground on which it stands? They say that the fungi feed on this decay; but surely not enough. And the amount in evaporation doesn't seem likely to be equivalent to the deposit, and we cannot say that as much has been taken from the earth in order to make the leaves as is given by their fall, since they take huge supplies also from the air. They weave the atmosphere into visible shape. On a single oak-tree seven million leaves have been counted. These leaves hang there throughout the country in perpetual slight motion in the ever-moving air, and by the conjured labours of millions of pores the substance of whole forests of solid wood is slowly extracted from the fleeting winds. Every year it rains heavily, it rains leaves, these leaves woven from the winds. Why is there not a mountainous result quite soon where there are woods? This question may be stupid, but I do not find that the answers I have ever received are very good.

Another thing. Why do we not notice a great change of air in the summer from what it was in the winter? There are those leaves extracting that vast amount of gas from the air, a process not active in winter, and yet we do not seem to suffer from it, do not notice any difference. Again, this question may seem too obviously the mark of an uninstructed mind; but I am relieved to find that Mr. H. E. Bates says that this very thing does affect him personally. 'It is as though—perhaps actually because—the air has been sucked up by a million leaves.' And he goes on to say (in *Through The Wood*), 'W. H. Hudson himself noticed this and had some comments on it in relation to the New Forest, where he felt that the great expanse of trees seemed to suck up all life and leave the mind and body and spirit as flabby as a sponge. He pointed out how pale the Hampshire people of that district looked, as though they were literally robbed of air.'

But one does not raise such questions with much hope of replies from specialists. They are far better at naming things than in answering questions of interest. If they can name a problem they often think they have solved it. 'Perhaps nothing is more curious in the history of the human mind', said Ruskin, 'than the way in which the science of botany has become oppressed with nomenclature.' Thus do they overcome the problems of reality by simply labelling reality, just as in other departments the significance of a man's point of view, his truth in which he passionately believes, is side-stepped by a label—his truth becoming merely an -ism. Still, I do not worry myself about getting answers to my questions. I rather like not getting them. And I can truthfully say that the phenomenon itself is good enough for me. Gazing upon phenomena, I find that my problems are not solved; but they are dissolved.

And of all phenomena concerning trees, that which appeals to me most is—the trunk. For me the most beautiful sight in the woods is not

the foliage, not the flowers, not the squirrel, not the deer—it is the trunks of trees of about thirty years old upwards. Especially the ash: the smooth grey bark; then a patch of dark moss; above it a patch of pale-green lichen in beautiful filigree pressed against the bark; then a number of white spots; then bark again; then moss again—no pattern, yet all pattern, no design yet all design, making a rounded tapestry beyond all the powers of art to render. No bright colours yet many colours—and in winter-time how often we see from the train window, tree-trunks almost as green as grass set in the gloom of the leafless boughs, taking the rain and the dusk in silent alertness. Once, having been given four freshly cut logs of silver birch, I did not burn them (in any case they wouldn't have been good as fire), but put them on a shelf as pictures. And I assure you they held my attention for many a day. Often I have been glad that I am not a painter; never more so than when confronted by some magnificent tree-trunk. Here is something that cannot be told, cannot be rendered. Here is the object, the thing itself, so staggering in its presence that we fall back from it, the intricacy of the totality cannot be copied, and it is the intricacy that is the picture; before it the art of suggestion is powerless, only the lower art of photography can give the total sum of the minutiae. Look at that old silver-birch trunk: knuckled, knotched, and dented with its ditches, ruts, and causeways, all subservient to the majesty of design; look at the splashes of smooth white irregularly placed, the bark itself, not lichen: if a house-painter did a post with dabs of white here and there like that we would think it a poor, strange piece of work: but here it is magnificent, the impression of the Whole is terrific—we must leave our pen, our brush in face of it, abandon art as a hopeless substitute. Look at that old Scotch pine-tree. It has no lichen, all the beauty is in the bark alone: rubbed, fluted, seamed, deeply chiselled, it is a personality, it is a Being. Perhaps that's what I'm after here in these fumbling words: the power and the glory here is in the *substance* of the thing, and art is without substance.

Truly trees are Beings. We feel that to be so. Hence their silence, their indifference to us is almost exasperating. We would speak to them, we would ask their message; for they seem to hold some weighty truth, some special secret—and though sometimes we receive their blessing, they do not answer, they make no sign. When we look upon a man we find that he is not satisfied, he wishes he were something else, or had done something else. When we look upon a monkey we see that clearly it is a lost soul. When we look upon a sheep we see that it is unhappy in itself. When we look upon a cow we cannot be certain that underneath its apparent calm it is not concealing a great unease.

Whitman said that he could turn and live with the animals. I would not join him. But many men have turned and lived with trees. They are much more companionable than cows. Thoreau would sometimes refuse to make an engagement with a friend on the ground that he had 'an appointment with a tree'. What then is their final appeal, their message to mankind? Isaac Rosenberg alone has told it.

> Then spake I to the tree,
> Were ye your own desire
> What is it ye would be?
> Answered the tree to me,
> I am my own desire;
> I am what I would be.

22. FIREWOOD

WHILE carrying out my business of thinning the wood I piled up the thick poles which I had cut down, in batches of a hundred—for, working by the piece, I made so much per lug and so much per hundred poles. These piles of poles made a very satisfactory sight for me, since they were carried away at intervals to be used as firewood in the neighbouring village, superb firewood at that. It gave me considerable pleasure to know that one result of my work up here was that I supplied wood for a whole village throughout the winter. At irregular periods it was carted away by Reggie and the boys. I would hear his high voice from a long way off, shouting at the horse, and about half an hour later they would arrive with the trailer which they used for loading up.

One of the reasons why I am especially attracted by ash is because it has so much fire in it. That may not be the proper way to put it; but it certainly seems as if flame resides inside the wood. When we have *put fire* to wood, what do we see? We do not see the fire *devouring* the wood as it goes along: we see the wood *becoming fire*, 'bursting into flames' as we say. Everything has fire in it, we are told, even stones—though it takes much extra heat to set a stone on fire. Of all the receptacles of fire in the world, wood is the most famous and our debt to it without measure. It is easy to understand how the ancient Aryans regarded trees as the *storerooms* of heat and that the sun itself was periodically recruited from the fire which resided in the sacred oak.

And of all trees, Ash becomes fire best. It need not be seasoned first, it burns almost equally well whether dry or cut down yesterday. If you cut down a bundle of fresh, green ash-twigs they do perfectly for lighting your fire, they are ready-made crackers, they are children's fireworks. Try the same thing with hazel and you'll never get your fire lit at all. Whenever I go to any new place in the country I look round at once to see if there are any ash woods nearby, for if so I know that I need not depend upon dry twigs for lighting fires. To my amazement I found many woodmen ignorant of this, while one or two who were not ignorant of it gave me surprising examples of wasteful folly caused by such ignorance. Observing the old man who worked with Reggie and the boys, taking home some hazel-faggots for his fire when there were heaps of ash around, I asked him why. He simply said that he had always done so. The fact that he had always done so was advanced in terms of a scientific statement that hazel made as good faggots as ash.

I used to take home a pole every day from the wood, and thus I was always in command of a magnificent fire—costing me nothing save the labour of carriage. Then the bitter cold of a winter's evening was transformed by the white-hot wood and I was nearly as happy in front of this earthly flame as in the summer under the sun.

I need not say that this job stimulated my interest in the financial aspect of fire-logs. All of us here were paid as woodmen, so much a week, or so much the piece; but occasionally I became familiar with the other sort of woodmen who, working on their own, made a good deal more by simply extracting wood and selling it—without any interest in the plantation. They made more, but of course they had to work hard for it, and to take risks. The man who really makes big profits is the man at the far end who distributes it—the man who neither plants, thins, tends, or extracts the wood. When I learnt the surprising prices charged for a sack of logs in the neighbouring towns, I realized that if you want to get rich in modern society you should not aim at securing the Means of Production, but rather the Means of Distribution. For to-day it is written—Blessed is he who distributes.

23. WINTER SCENES: THE CALAMITY

I LOOKED forward during the day to my superb evening fires in the winter months. It is not often very cold in a wood even when it is biting outside, in fact the difference in temperature on the same day in the wood as against the field, is sometimes phenomenal. Nevertheless there were spells when my hands were too cold to grip the axe and the wind so keen that no amount of work served to make me warm. At such times I wanted to get away from the wood—though not into any other agricultural job.

Often it was merely damp, windless, and dreary. At such times I felt curiously lonely amongst the trees, in a pleasantly sad sort of way. The silence was so melancholy, the mystery of the trees and the dark undergrowth so great, that I felt exiled from truth as well as from mankind. I used to grope my way in explorations into the deeper darknesses beyond my immediate position, peering round with something of the expectancy and the fear of a man in a haunted house.

I frequently came upon fresh examples of fallen trunks lying on the ground in various stages of decomposition: there were some great hulks whose outer crust was as soft as earth, and whose inner caverns, on being exposed by the bill-hook, revealed curious insects curled up here and there in holes evidently intended as dormitories for the winter. That was one type; but there was another I almost preferred—the long trunk, sunk low, covered with moss and leafage, becoming indistinguishable from the ground as it tapered to what was once its top. I had one favourite of this kind. It was considerably long: the thickest end was like a mound, and it gradually tapered on getting smaller and smaller until it became level with the ground, and only the freshness of the moss showed me where the 'wood' was. And if I walked along upon this strange rise, it was exactly as if I were walking upon something as soft as a mountain swamp.

The moss was deep and clear upon these barks. It was also laid across the whole floor of the wood. In the winter one becomes conscious of this new glory. When the spring flowers are long forgotten and the new series is in hidden preparation out of sight and of thought; when the bracken that rose so high and green has browned and fallen down; when the herb-willow has posted its final envelope of seed; when the latest storm has removed the last leaves from tree and bush; when the long, low kingdom of dog's mercury has disappeared—then the ground is not bare, it is not desolate: it shines again with a new growth; we enter the reign of moss. This is one of the sweetest and dearest of all plants. We think of it in the mass and speak of winding mossy ways, as so we should; but if we look close we see that it is a network of the most delicate little fronds whose massed formations give us the soft, deep carpet. It is not seen during the summer, and where we do discern it, it is parched and poor; but in the chill of winter when all other life is in abeyance this is in the ascendant, the floor of the earth is cushioned and all the scars of mortality are bandaged and made blessed.

During the short winter days I sometimes arrived in the wood while the moon was still the only light, and day had not yet broken in. At this hour, before the particular beam of the sun had changed the scene, the atmosphere was expectant. Nature appeared to be listening carefully for something and was evidently awaiting some great event. I did not dare say a word, even to cough. Objects which in the light of day were animated only with the life of plants, became informed with the life of beasts, so that mere bushes looked like tigers about to spring. When the day broke in at last it did not do so slowly as it is supposed to do in these climes, there came a moment when the darkness began to lighten up quite steadily and swiftly. The moon started to go out as if someone were turning down a lamp rather gingerly, and the light of the hidden sun illuminated the scene almost at the rate of theatrical lights slowly bathing a stage that had been in darkness.

At other times, arriving on a misty morning, I found that the wood was of immense size, receding into the distance on all sides as if it were boundless in space and belonging to any Age. The boles of the trees, erect in the mist, were as thin and pale as the pencillings in a Chinese drawing. They had no strength or substance: it would have been easy to rub them all out of the picture. As the day advanced and the sun rose to cancel the morning mist, the scene shifted. The Present Day came back again, the wood occupied a given number of acres, the trees were hard and firm once more. Then the afternoon sun was turned upon them, and they held the light, they stopped it and took it upon themselves, each a shining post, while the wind blew and the strange, unhappy hours passed by—for even in a wood at this time of the day, more so in a wood than elsewhere when the wind blows unceasingly, all solitary men are perplexed and feel the motion of infelicity.

These were days when a hot drink was the very thing in the course of the morning, and I never forgot to bring out my thermos-flask. Its cap was broken, lacking which I generally brought a china cup with me. But sometimes I forgot this item. However, I had a remedy when this happened. At this time of the year many more varieties of fungi attracted my attention. There was one species which particularly appealed to me. It was pale yellow and shaped like a large wine-glass. On the occasions when I forgot to bring out my cup I simply plucked one of these stalked cups made of fungus, filled it from my thermos-flask, and thus had my drink in comfort.

It was not possible to do much work in the intense cold nor in heavy rain. When it rained slightly it was quite all right, and many a time when I should have had to seek shelter if in the fields, I could carry on in the wood without a raincoat. But a continuously wet day made it impossible (especially earlier in the year when the leaves were still on the trees, for then your stroke brought down a great deal of extra water upon you) for the axe then became too slippery to hold. When it snowed my work stopped immediately, of course. I have often referred here to the silences peculiar to the woodman's life; but is there any silence so deep and rare as that bestowed by snow? Whether in a wood, or outside, it is a wonderful thing in our machine age to find the world in the morning ankle-deep in snow. Then the unwonted silence that falls upon our life is truly magnificent; and when the snow has been really heavy making all lanes and many roads impassable, the sense of isolation in our silence carries us right back to the days when communication even between villages was scarce and chequered. One

heavy fall of snow in the country, and modern civilization is *silenced*!

These winter scenes are related in my mind with another scene, more human and more sad. Reggie occasionally came across from his part of the estate to see me. I think of a certain Friday when I heard him call my name (he used my Christian name), and appeared coming through the trees with his dog and his gun, which he often carried. He had some agricultural extra clothing-coupons to give me, and brought a paper for me to sign. And then we fell into conversation about this and that, his early life in Devon, the present life here, the wages young boys got nowadays and what they did with the money, his rank of Corporal in the Home Guard, and so on. He draped himself against a tree as usual, his remarkable flaxen hair, his brown face, and workman's clothes fitting into the surroundings perfectly and, indeed, beautifully. Thus we stood and talked upon the general affairs of life, amongst the friendly trees, well cornered from the rough traffic of the world, far away from the great battles that were then being fought, insensible in this leafy harbour to the noise and rumour of the field, secure from calamity and the sudden dart of death, or so it seemed. Presently he went away. He called to his little genteel black dog, and disappeared through the trees out of my sight, and went across a field towards the scene of his death. For he was never to return along these ways nor would that voice be heard in the woods any more. Later in the afternoon there was a dreadful explosion, louder and more earth-shaking than others I had heard in the neighbourhood, due to the practising soldiery. This explosion was not made by the army. Reggie had picked up a bomb which he imagined was quite harmless. He had brought it back to his shed. He thought it was a smoke-bomb of some sort and decided to examine its interior. Finding it difficult to dismantle, he took a hammer and began to tap it. The boys, who were standing near, became frightened and tried to dissuade him; but he sat there bending over the bomb, tapping at it. It exploded, blowing his hands off and killing him—the boys escaping death, but not injury.

The whole village shuddered at this meaningless tragedy. The catastrophe of our time was focused upon the body of this one man, cut down suddenly in the midst of abounding life.

24. FAREWELL TO THE WOOD

In the company of flowers we know happiness. In the company of trees we are able to *think*, they foster meditation. Trees are very intellectual. There is nowhere on earth we can think so well as in a thin wood resting against a tree. Such at least is my experience, and it is the ultimate memory that I shall carry away from this place. For in parting I know that the greatest wrench of all is in connection with the old oak-tree (under which or in the vicinity of which I have written this account). It is not easy to say farewell to it; not easy to pass from the best spot in the whole world between the hours of eight and ten in the morning during May and August. For, as I have said, that is the time when the sun rested upon my seat.

Sometimes I could wish that my love of the sun were less genuine. How often I have felt compelled to alter my plans for the day's work because the sun unexpectedly came out to shine against my special tree or on some other favourite spot! I have been about to do a portion of thinning marked out as the minimum for the morning, when, the sun coming out, I have abandoned my schedule in order to seize, if only for a few cloud-chequered intervals, the gift of the sun at that hour, in that blessed place. I have had to turn back for the same reason, while on my way into the neighbouring town to get some much-needed things. The sun deflects me from my courses. I mention this as the kind of psychological fact that holds a certain interest, since we scarcely allow enough for the part such things play in the destinies of men. I often wonder at anyone accepting the Materialistic Conception of History. Many people, after Marx, began to say that circumstances are